Phonetics and Spoken English

Phonetics and Spoken English

Edited by

D. Murali Manohar

7/22, Ansari Road, Darya Ganj, New Delhi
Tel.: +91-11-4077 5252, 2327 3880
E-mail: orders@atlanticbooks.com
Web: www.atlanticbooks.com

Reprinted in 2026, 2025

Published by Atlantic Publishers & Distributors (P) Ltd.

Printed & bound in India by Atlantic Print Services

Dedicated to

My father Dasari Obanna and
My mother Dasari Laxmi Devi,
who have
Reached the soul of Lord Krishna

Acknowledgements

I would like to thank Prof. Sachidananda Mohanty, Head, Department of English, University of Hyderabad, Hyderabad for approving and encouraging me to organize the seminar with the fund which is available within the department. I am grateful to Prof. Mohan Ramanan, Dean, School of Humanities, for initiating the seminar with funds and encouraging academic activities.

I would like to thank my friends who have chaired the sessions successfully during the seminar. The friends are: Prof. Pingali Sailaja, Prof. Sachidananda Mohanty, Prof. Mohan Ramanan, Dr. C. Murali Krishna, Dr. Sunita Mishra, Dr. Anand Mahanand, Dr. P. Hari Padma Rani and Dr. Rajyam Rama.

I also need to thank my friends Prof. Alladi Uma and Dr. Sunita Mishra for their moral and academic support.

I must thank all the participants for submitting full papers in order that I could compile a draft of the proceedings and approach the publisher. I am indebted to Dr. K.R. Gupta the Honorary Advisor of Atlantic Publishers and Distributors (P) Ltd., who takes extreme care in bringing out best quality books with superior paper, not to mention the excellent cover design.

D. Murali Manohar

Contents

Introduction

This book is a compilation of papers presented at the national seminar on "Phonetics and Spoken English" held on 30-31 October 2009 at University of Hyderabad, Hyderabad. The participants were from across the country, from the areas of Andhra Pradesh, Karnataka, Maharashtra, Orissa and Puducherry.

I had observed that many English teachers, whether they are in schools or in colleges or in universities, are not confident of teaching phonetics of English. Also there has been a debate on what should be the curriculum in Spoken English Institutes. There are two papers in this book, on Spoken English Institutes, by Sharda Acharya and Trishna Kar, and Mr. E. Vijaya Raghava.

There are specific papers in this volume on the teaching of Phonetics, by V. Prasad from Puducherry (Pondicherry), P. Hari Padma Rani from Tirupati (Andhra Pradesh), Durga Prasad Dash from Rajam (Andhra Pradesh), Mallikarjunappa from Bellary (Karnataka), and Dyvadatham from Kuppam (Andhra Pradesh).

Sudhakar Marathe starts with day-to-day examples and moves on to the literary texts of writers as varied as Nevil Shute, George MacDonald Fraser, Gerard Manley Hopkins, John Milton and William Shakespeare, which can be used to improve "Phonetics". He would rather use the word "Speech" instead of "Phonetics". Speech is important because students imitate teachers just as children imitate their parents. Knowledge is power, and so is language. However, according to Prof. Sudhakar Marathe, "Spoken language has enormously greater power because it is versatile and direct."

My own paper on "Teaching the Phonetics of English: Case Studies" reveals that many of the English teachers in schools, colleges and universities are not confident enough to teach Phonetics. The reason could be that they did not show interest in it and had never thought of teaching it in future. I have arrived at this conclusion based on my teaching the students who expressed that they are not even aware of it. The teachers who taught English did not teach Phonetics/Speech (to borrow Sudhakar's word), at all levels.

Continuing the Navodaya Vidyalaya teaching experience is V. Prasad who is still in the Navodaya system unlike me. He has a paper in which he shares his happy moments and agonies in teaching those young students, covering all the language skills, including Phonetics, stress, and intonation and identifying the problems of the students considering the background they come from. Within the limitations of the system he is doing a wonderful job with lots of enthusiasm and energy. I am glad that he took Phonetics seriously and is able to teach without any difficulty. He agrees with me that many students throw challenges to the teachers, especially in Phonetics.

Influence of the mother tongue is one of the problems in teaching Phonetics. With a lot of examples and quoting from across the country, Durga Prasad Dash identifies many of these problems in his paper. He is of the view that students learn Speech only at an advanced level. But are the students responsible for this? Or are the teachers responsible for this because they are not confident enough to teach them at school level? If the seeds of English speech sounds are sown at the early level, perhaps the advanced level students would not face the existing problems. Students have been very critical about not having an exam system for Speech, lack of proficient teachers to teach Speech, lack of courses and institutes to teach Speech. Finally he is of the opinion that we do not have uniform syllabus for English, which causes this problem.

As against the influence of the mother tongue, World English, according to Sharda Acharya and Trishna Kar, is the status that the English language has attained with the help mainly of the British Broadcasting Corporation. This paper has to do with a review of what Spoken English institutes such as British Council, Institute of English and Foreign Languages (IEFL), EFLU, Hira Spoken English, VETA offer such as "Keep Talking", "Spoken English Skills", and "Enhance Your English" catering to each individual's level of proficiency whether he/she is at primary, intermediate or advanced level.

Susanto's paper is very practical and addresses directly the theme of the seminar. It is not an ongoing research but an experiment with students. His case study is on five adult Indonesian students for his experiment on the place of articulation within nasal sounds. The paper has been sharply focused and has shown the pictures with acoustic features. He has also provided the spectrograms of nasal sounds.

A. Mallikarjunappa, like Susanto, talks about an experiment for which he has prepared a questionnaire consisting of 16 questions. The questions were framed on vowels, consonants, diphthongs, accent, stress, pronunciation, etc. and distributed to a few engineering colleges, one medical college and a couple of management colleges to know how much awareness the teachers and students have of spoken English. The target students were high school students consisting of English convent schools, government-aided schools and government schools. Fifty-four teachers responded to the questionnaire. According Mallikarjunappa's survey, 75 per cent teachers are not trained in Phonetics of English. This is what is troublesome. How can we blame students if they make mistakes when teachers themselves are not trained in Phonetics? English teachers are appointed based on their fluency in English language but not based on their command of the language aspects of Speech. That is where the problem lies.

While Sharda Acharya and Trishna Kar advocate "World English", Sreedevi advocates "Global English" which is similar. Software companies, multinational companies, etc. spend a lot of money training their employees in English such as pronunciation, accent and stress and it has been mandatory for them to survive and accelerate the company in satisfying the global clients. The non-native speakers have the patience in understanding the pronunciation of English. Moreover, they bring in local idioms into English with direct translation, which confuses the native speakers. After making these points, Sreedevi goes on to discuss the predicament of BPOs and software companies in India in these areas.

Tracing the roots of English establishing itself in the people's mind since Macaulay's Minute, Arun Kumar Mishra begins his paper in order to show how Standard English has been replaced by Indian English. Though a few people speak English in India, it has occupied the fourth place in the world scenario. Mishra's study is an experiment carried out with the recording at the levels of phonology, morphology, and lexical influence of Hindi in words and sentences. The Indian English is also used for fun. At the same time, use of English attains respect and status of a snob.

Before making critique of English teachers at JNTU and other Engineering college teachers who are unable to teach the basic things of Speech mechanism, stress and intonation, Arabati Pradeep Kumar defines communication and explains its importance at all levels for opportunities. While describing the Speech mechanism Pradeep also defines what GIE, RP and American model are. He also suggests that these days the American model is also preferred. However, due to historical reasons, RP is being followed. Pradeep's main concern in this paper is about the non-relation with the letters and sounds which would create confusion among those who are familiar with the Speech mechanism. He cites examples for each of them such as same letters having different sounds; single sound for double letters; and demonstrates the idea in an effective way. The second part of his paper is about word and sentence stress which are very important for conversation. The last part of his paper is on intonation.

Mousumi Dash and Monalisa Mishra conduct experiment with the BPO and software companies where English plays a major role in handling the clients. If the employees are not good at English, they are to undergo training. They collect opinion on Phonetics and try to suggest company employees to overcome difficulties in pronouncing the vowels, consonants, glides/diphthongs, with appropriate examples. This paper aims at bringing out the missing links and formidable gaps that are created during a corporate transaction or an outsourcing effort and focuses on identifying the problems. Having identified the problems, they feel that we will be able to avoid any sort of confusion at workplace, thereby understand others and being understood correctly. This will help us to create a common platform on which Indian speakers can pronounce the sounds of English, where the receiver understands and decodes the ideas exactly as they are encoded by the sender.

Jayanth Kasyap, in his paper, discusses about the use of software for Phonetics and spoken English through the language laboratory to teach English. In a way, the teacher becomes a mere facilitator and intervenes occasionally when the students go wrong. The learner has to be evaluated whether he/she can be taken to the lab for study. Is the learner equipped enough to be part of lab learning? Kasyap also talks about the advantages and limitations of lab use in English Language Teaching (ELT).

E. Vijaya Raghava shares his experiences as the teacher and director of his own institute in teaching spoken English to students coming from varied backgrounds. The demands and expectations of students are with no correspondence. Each client has his/her demands in the course. He also shares his objective, motto and purpose of running the institute and the methodology that he adopts to teach English to his students.

Srinivasa Kumar Kolusu conducts the experiment and shares his findings with us about the Call Centre representatives pronouncing certain words, by visiting the BPOs based in Hyderabad. In his research, he discovers that the nature of sentence construction, accent, pronunciation, diction, the use of vocabulary, listening and reading comprehension—all pose a challenge to an American or a British customer in understanding Indian English. Hence, he identifies the grammatical and phonological errors and offers suggestions to improve upon them.

Teaching is one aspect which includes delivering lectures and trying to know how many students follow the lectures. Anand Mahanand and Suchismita Barik, in their paper entitled "Difficulties Faced by MA English Students in Comprehending Lectures", address this concern. They distributed a questionnaire to 20 MA English students coming from both rural and urban backgrounds to extract the information and analyze the data and provide their observations. One of the suggestions they made is to deliver lectures in a comprehensible accent so that everyone understands them. This paper also reminds us of Hari Padma Rani's teaching experience of her MA students using the RP accent and the students laughing as the accent is very peculiar to them.

Teaching pronunciation, that too correct pronunciation, is what concerns R. Dyvadatham in his paper. He reminds us that we should not get confused about sound and the letter. He also deals with some aspects of pronunciation and communication which are interrelated. With this assumption he asks a research question as to how pronunciation helps in developing and improving communication skill. He chooses postgraduate students who come from Telugu medium background and have no exposure to Phonetics. Due to lack of knowledge, they mispronounce the words. He has chosen 60 words and conducted an experiment with them for 30 days by recording their speech. Dyvadatham also stresses in his paper that a knowledge of Phonetics is essential for the teacher if the situation is to improve.

If Dyvadatham experiments with English words and their pronunciation with his students in order to improve communication skills, Bhujanga Reddy experiments with the sound system of two languages such as English and Telugu. His paper is interesting because he takes the two languages, compares their sound system and shows the differences between their sounds and sound symbols. While talking about the sounds, he also points out differences in the consonant sounds, sequence of consonant clusters, geminated sounds and goes further to show the distribution of consonants and representation of sounds.

While many of the paper readers did not concentrate on RP, and Indian English accent, Sridhar Maisa gives importance to RP and he compares this with GAE (General American English) (Pradeep Kumar uses it as a passing reference) by giving many examples. This paper focuses on the American accent which is playing a significant role in getting jobs in BPO and multinational companies (Sreedevi, Sharda Acharya and Trishna Kar do point out this fact). In fact, MA English students get immediate jobs thanks to the RP and GAE.

Hari Padma Rani directly addresses the teaching of Phonetics and tries to analyse why it is very hard for a teacher to succeed. Who is responsible for this? One might say it is the teacher, and another might say it is the education system that is responsible. The postgraduate students come from an Indian language medium background and face difficulties in learning from the teacher who has been trying hard to teach Phonetics to his/her students. She also makes a valid point that there is no oral test for the students to learn Phonetics. Both Hari Padma and Durga Prasad Dash advocate that Phonetics should have the component of oral exam.

In my earlier paper I had discussed like Hari Padma, about teaching Phonetics of English, whereas in the paper entitled "Reading and Writing: A Case Study of Success in ESL Classroom and CBSE Board Exams", I have covered reading and writing skills which help students to get better grades in CBSE Board exams. It was an experiment at Jawahar Navodaya Vidyalaya, Pabbra, Hisar District, Haryana (like Sreedevi and Dash) which tested all the four skills of Listening, Speaking, Reading and Writing. I could succeed in developing all the four skills in the students within two years of my teaching. The method of teaching that I had adopted was Direct Method which has been critiqued for not working in a bilingual country like ours. However, I could succeed with this method. With dedication, despite adverse comments from some quarters, one could make one's students progress in basic skills.

In his article "English Pronunciation and Spelling: Mysteries and Revelations", Panchanan Mohanty strongly advocates a standard Indian English after the existence of

American English, Australian English, Canadian English and Japanese English. Arun Kumar Mishra too touches upon Indian English in his paper. A lot of research is being done on Indian English. There are problems with the regional accents with which many people pronounce English in India.

Mohanty distinguishes between intake and input. Teaching is an input which has to be converted into an intake by the students. Otherwise, teaching has no value. He also talks about the peculiarities of spelling and their pronunciation which create confusion. A proper discussion has to take place in order to understand stress with heavy syllable and light syllable. Mohanty advocates students discovering rules from a lot of examples rather than the teachers imposing rules on students.

This book will be useful to those scholars who are working on Speech and Phonetics. This book may also be useful to those who run Spoken English institutes. This may help them in paying more attention to important issues.

D. Murali Manohar

1

Who Needs to Worry about Spoken English!

Sudhakar Marathe

One of my general and oft repeated experiences will do nicely to begin our discussion regarding the subject encapsulated in my title. Many a time I have used a very dramatic poem as material for discussion in refresher courses for college and university teachers of English. It is the sort of poem that ought to be prescribed for reading in general language classes, special language—study classes and literature classes. It provides exciting opportunities for verbal rendering and interpretation. Its first line, beginning in the middles of a dramatic situation, and perfectly ordinary in idiomatic English, turns out to be magical, a shibboleth, a test of teachers' ability in both their mother tongues (or their students' tongues) and their English. What virtually every tested teacher fails to do symbolizes the essence of the answer to the pseudo or rhetorical question in my title. So let us begin with it. The poem, which reports one side of a particularly animated series of conversations, begins in the middle of the action with the following line:

> Of course you can play with them....

as if someone had just asked a person, "May we play with these words, please?"

Since most college teachers trade heavily upon the true or conveniently perceived fact in a large number of India's schools and colleges that everyone expects them to teach English in their students' mother tongue, which is also the teachers' mother tongue in nine cases out of ten, I ask them to translate the poem in it as they would have to do for teaching. This is how they translate the opening line, for instance, in Hindi and Marathi, but in fact they produce clones of these lines in all their mother tongues;

Arthat / zarur ap unke sath khel sakte hein.
arthat tumhi tyanchyashi khelu shakta.

When I ask them to read their translations out to their peers, being teachers, they not only hesitate but also eventually read their creations in a pedagogically typical *lifeless* manner, as follows:

arthat / zarur ap unke sath khel sakte hein...
arthat tumhi tyanchyashi khelu shakta...

I tell them bluntly that even corpses would read or render the lines with greater animation! Not only are such translations and renderings *utterly* unnatural in Hindi and Marathi, but they are also always delivered with total disregard of the *spoken* idiom of the *mother tongues*: of course you will realize that both *mother* and *tongues* are particularly significant words in this context. And I know that teachers deliver the line just as lifelessly in English also:

Of course you can play with them....

Now, most ordinary citizens of the world believe that speech has nothing to do with idiom. That is fine, really, because unlike us they do not cogitate and theorise and quarrel about language at leisure or in seminars and conferences or write articles on the subject. Ordinary members of a language community are happy enough to *possess* a language! But we *in the language business* cannot afford to forget *even for a moment* that in reality speech has as much to do with idiom, grammar, discourse, style and propriety as individual turn of phrase and speech in a language that expresses what your brain conceives and your heart feels. Speech has as much to do with idiom at all levels of language as your heart has to do with your brain. No one in his right mind would ever compose lines like those my teacher audiences do in Hindi or Marathi, or

Swahili, Tagalog or Bahasa Indonesia; no one would be caught dead (to pun on the word deliberately) delivering them in such an utterly lifeless manner. First of all, in choice of diction and grammar the Hindi translation would *have* to be

han, han, khelo, khelo!

or some version of that phrasing and a Marathi translation would *have* to be like

hoooooo, khelaki!

As a matter of fact, human languages are far more dramatic in their spoken *avatars* even in perfectly ordinary circumstances than English teachers ever seem to imagine. Moreover, each version would have to be delivered with as much life and vigour as the circumstances of hidden story in the poem requires:

han, han, khelo, khelo!
hoooooo, khelaki!

Not only will the spoken utterance be on the lines which have been mentioned above, but certain body postures and gestures characteristic of each language will also accompany its delivery. The pernicious mischief in all our second-language classes—whether in English as a second language or Telugu as a second language or the Hindi lessons 'kindly' offered to Americans in the Study India Programme of the University of Hyderabad—comprise *masking* the fundamental fact that language is a *multi-media performance*, never a "dead-letter" text. Even in its printed form, like a photograph of your beloved or the proverbial ripe apple hanging on a tree and *waiting* to fall, it has *potential energy*, it is *live* and *vital.* And language is absolutely nothing if it is not vital. It is the manifestation of its incipient or potential power that makes language such a species defining property of the human race, unique on this earth at least. To forget this fundamental truth or to treat it with contempt in mind and act is tantamount to matricide. Those who forget the truth have their heads buried in sand, although one is tempted to use the vulgar yet apt American slang version I dare not use here!

Now, first of all we must assert two other fundamental facts. Whether we consider English an Indian language or not, it is a mother tongue for almost no one in India but always a *second* language; and no matter which language one is attempting to learn as a second language, English or Tamil or Malayalam, speech ought to remain the primary concern of the whole extended pedagogic process, *even* in classes in writing skills. No matter what language, whether one's first language or second, third or fourth, to neglect its speech, to neglect the not just essential but actually *umbilical* connection of speech to language, is to treat it in the shabbiest possible manner. Not only do we indulge in more speech than writing in virtually any language we use; not only does speech dominate a teacher's life, and the life of anyone who studies or uses a language beyond the most basic of courses; but those of you who have had the least brush with the science of language *must* also know that speech is *primary* at *four* points in its history, in the strong and literal meaning of the word primary: first, speech is primary in the history of virtually every *natural* human language; it appears that even in deliberately constructed languages like Esperanto, Aficionados make every effort to speak it as though it were a natural language. And writing is so very recent in human civilization that in the history of the race speech is the primary stage of linguistic expression; second, in every person's existence in his mother tongue, speech is learned first and even today writing may not be learned at all; third, even when one has mastered it, virtually all our conduct in our mother tongue is in the form of speech; and fourth, in the conduct of the lives of most people who learn a second language for use such as English, speech is both the primary and the ultimate form of the language. Indeed, writing is very much the poorer for not being able to embody the power of its spoken version: it is like the printed menu at a restaurant that serves fabulous food of some region, food that simply cannot be imagined in flavour and taste even from their colourful names in an unknown language, but must be tasted. Of course, that is and ought to be our understanding of very language we learn as second language. Not to teach speech is to deprive students of all linguistic vitality. And English is only a token for the whole type called second language in both learning and teaching as a second language.

As for English teachers in India, with a few exceptions among university teachers, virtually none of them writes more than a few sentences everyday, but everyone of them speaks 60 words a minute in his classes, class after class, day after day, week after week, year after year, decade after decade. Naturally, and we need not qualify this claim, most of his students learn how to speak English from the *way* in which *he* speaks the language. Indeed, those especially interested in the culture embodied in language ought to pay special attention to how it is spoken; because only a small proportion of culture resides in words, the rest manifests itself in the way chains of words are actually uttered.

We may say with extraordinary charity that a teacher may not be aware of this fact or he may not appreciate its significance; he may be ignorant of his responsibility in the case, although if such is the case with any of us, we do not deserve to be employed as teachers. But even worse is the case of thousands of us who *know* that they are our students' *only* models for the spoken form of English, yet do not care a bit about how they speak the language. That is not just dereliction of duty but also gross neglect of the opportunity to impart the *power* of speech to students. And while as teachers we *may* be able to bestow many *other* kinds of favours upon our students, none is as great and as essential as the gift of speech. Forget this, and you participate in the nasty game of deprivation of students, deprivation of the power of expression and understanding that only speech can bestow on anyone. Yet from the first lesson in English in the kindergarten class or the fifth standard at school, to our B.A. and M.A. classes in language and literature alike, the soul of which is in the *heard* shape of writing, we blithely deprive our students.

While speech is thus all important, mastering it and teaching it by example (how can one teach or practise speech in theory!) teaching language altogether from its written *avatar* is the most readily escapist route for teachers. Writing is like a ghost, or like the photograph of a prospective spouse. I often ask teachers whether they first saw a photograph of the person they eventually married; many say yes; I then ask if they would have been happy marrying that photograph, they invariably and fervently answer, "Oh, no!" Yet they think there is nothing wrong with marrying their students off to two-dimensional, written versions of second languages like English! I have yet to meet a regular teacher of English who is proud to command its speech adequately. Most of us take recourse to some lame second-hand excuse to the effect that we need not really learn how to speak the language. Some make the excuse with a patriotic tinge while labouring under ignorance about the British colonial period or any other period in our history. But they would never make the same excuse if the second language were their own mother tongue! Even a passé if not dead language like Sanskrit needs to be uttered with effect and feeling, not like some kind of Braille for the sighted.

Language is power. And spoken language is enormously greater power because it is versatile and direct. That includes the ability to hear the language well; including nuances and variations of meaning and the ability to make variations in meaning at will even without changing the vocabulary one uses. No one denies the learning of running to his offspring. No one suggests that their mother tongue or speech had better remain flat and expressionless. No one would be satisfied with the frozen version of their mother tongue as recorded in black letters upon white paper. But in India, not only do we attempt to teach only the written form of the English language for use but we also teach literature in it yet without reference to the resuscitated, inflected, expressive spoken rendering of its written version.

A brief moment's thought will convince anyone that writing embodies a very small percentage of the whole sense of any bit of language, especially language as it is used in real life and therefore as it appears in literature, which is the imagined *avatar* of real life. Writing is as poor a copy as the photograph of one's spouse. Everyone wants a flesh and blood spouse, not a mere photograph. For the same reasons and for equally strong reasons, one must think of a second language as flesh and blood in its warm and throbbing spoken form. Sometimes people object to the teaching of speech because they believe not everyone needs it. Well, not only does everyone need it, at the B.A. and M.A. levels of study, but also everyone ought to acquire adequate command of speech in English. Traditionally, most persons are turning to teaching these days. But you would be *grossly* mistaken: today they go into the media, print media and audio-video media, and they do far greater damage as reporters, newscasters, anchors and editors because they reach and corrupt such vast audiences as teachers never did before. So many private institutions have opened that pretend to teach spoken English today; so many more millions of Indians are thirsting for command of spoken English today because that is the key to numerous kinds of modern jobs; so many millions today desire to impress others with their command of spoken English. Not even in fun can one say any longer what a pesky student of mine said, in my absence, in this very department- apparently a discussion happened in a class about why we need bother with teaching the theory and practice of English speech; and that student said, "Because Professor Marathe is here! Well, good luck to such cheek. But no amount of cheek can gainsay the fact that a good command of *versatile* spoken English has become increasingly more valuable today than ever before in India's British-colonial or post-British-colonial history.

Only a few weeks ago, at long last, the Government of Kerala apparently summoned enough gumption to admit in public that Malayali young people were unable to find worthwhile employment elsewhere in India in the newer lucrative firms *because* their spoken English was just not up to the mark! You know very well that in India a government only admits a tenth of any problem. So the problem must have assumed worrisome proportions for them to have admitted this reality. If the I.T. industry and International Service Industries had operated in Hindi, the government of Kerala would have had to make exactly the same conclusion. In a country where even in mother tongue education little care is given to the skill of speaking, although we have installed the Goddess of Speech Vani in our pantheon, how would you expect the people to realize the value of teaching our students how to speak

English? That is *our* job, in university departments and education colleges. For it is a power that must percolate downwards from the centres of what is erroneously called Higher Learning. This department realized over thirty years ago—even though a few of its faculty may not quite see the point today once again—that teaching speech had to be a priority in the curriculum. That is why courses in the discipline were introduced into the curriculum. But few realize that the awareness had come to some much earlier—for the professor who introduced the element of speech into the curriculum here had done so more than a decade previously in his department at the University of Poona. And that was not me, but Professor S. Nagarajan, who saw far in many directions in our discipline.

What, then, ought we to do about the teaching of English speech in our B.A., M.A. and B.Ed. and M.Ed. programmes not as merely theoretical discipline but a performance discipline? I know many a professor who gives "powerful" (second hand) lectures on how dramatic Shakespeare's plays are, how dramatic this or that speech is in his plays, so as I said once before elsewhere they learn that the *teacher* thinks *Hamlet* is a very *dramatic* play but they never do understand *why* he thinks so, for they cannot render the simplest of Shakespeare's speeches effectively. And they lecture with eloquence of sorts about how dramatic other texts are such as James Joyce's *Ulysses* or Tennyson's "The Lady of Shalott" or Nissim Ezekiel's "Night of the Scorpion". But even to save their lives they cannot *demonstrate* the drama in speeches in plays or such other texts! That is not necessarily because they have a poor understanding of drama, really, but because they have a poor command of English speech. Yet all the while they lecture, and thousands of other English teachers lecture, humbly or pompously as the case may be; and their stilted, idiomatically curious, erroneous or highly questionable speech in class becomes the model for their students. Poor students willy-nilly imitate whatever they hear.

And, unfortunately, since they still parrot the principle *Guru devo bhava*, they are happy to imitate the faulty models teachers present to them. There are odd exceptions, of course, these days you are far more likely to hear imitation American accents even in the corridors of this very building: "Hi, guys!" but not even a single line of effective speech besides parroted, or shall I say pirated, catch phrases. Nor is it a matter of not being able to utter one word here and another there, such as the word d-e-v-e-l-o-p, which most of us pronounce as DEV-lup. Many a polite foreigner says nothing on the spot in reaction to the confusion this mispronunciation causes. Later they take someone aside and ask earnestly, "Can you tell me what 'double up' means in *this* context?" The situation in India is indeed grave in terms of the degree of erroneousness in speech, both in pronunciation of analyzable elements such as words and phrases and in the expression of sentences and larger discourses. And yet everyone touts a species of language teaching horrifically titled Communicative English, as though English was ever meant to be *un*-communicative! Hardly anyone including language teachers seems to mind the difference between many of our languages and English, that the latter is stress-timed and without appropriate stress and intonation patterns it is reduced to mere strings of words, provided the words can be recognized.

Moreover, linguistic utterance enables one to infuse more meaning or different meaning into language that words *cannot* give it, nor can syntax. It is a question of possessing the power to emphasize or undercut or twist or enhance the meaning of the same words by uttering them in appropriately different ways. It is a power that we ought all to want to possess in any language we wish to command. This power is above words and strings of words and punctuation marks and sentence types. That is why knowing scholars call such speech phenomena "above" language broken up into constituent units, supra-segmental or applicable to a whole utterance and not just to one bit of it. It is the power of the spoken language—*any* language—that converts dead sentences, or at best moribund sentences, into vital communication capable of affecting meaning and relationships, of dealing with intimacy or formality, seriousness or humour, feeling and emotion and subtle degrees of all of these. One needs to know that to ask someone, "Would you like some tea?" with a falling intonation is an act of near rudeness in English. Yet most of us are incapable of being routinely polite in English and ask "the same" question with a rising intonation, "Would you like some tea?" nor can we be knowingly rude if necessary by uttering the same question on a low and growling near-monotone, as in "Would you like some tea?" Yet one might learn such power even from children's story books, for instance *The Elephant and the Bad Baby*, in which the polite elephant asks an impolite baby repeatedly questions such as, "Would you like an apple?" or "Would you like a lollipop?" and the Bad baby is punished in a token manner for repeatedly giving the rude answer, "Yes," instead of the idiomatically appropriate answer, "Yes, please!" Everything in language has potential power that becomes dynamic power when we speak. But that power remains unmanifested unless we command the skills of speaking that manifest it in actual utterances. And in any case why bother to learn a language if one is *not* after *all* the power it can give a *prasadam*? Do not for a moment think that knowing how to speak a language relates only to speaking. One cannot even read a written text in it with its full meaning and impact without hearing it with one's eyes as one reads! That is right to claim that one genuinely commands a language implies that one is able to see it with one's ears and hear it with one's eyes. Only then will a text in real life or on a page acquire the many dimensions it is meant to possess.

Unfortunately, factionalism is our chief professional philosophy in India. Organizations whose job it was to integrate all aspects of the teaching of English have actually widened the gap. Consequently those who seem to deal with literature in their classes consider themselves superior to those who are expected to teach language. And those who teach language consider themselves some sort of superior *scientific* species and think of literature teachers as an inferior species given to subjectivism. Each wants to thump his chest with Sinful Pride and feel, like Shakespeare's Coriolanus, "Alone I did it!" But in fact a language teacher who does not know how to realize the power of the written word *including* the literary word, or a literature teacher who does not regularly and as a matter of *course* analyze the language, including its spoken form, in *every* text he teaches, falls far short of delivering the goods they are supposed to deliver. One ought to foster and cherish a significant mutual cooperation between these childishly distinguished branches of our profession. So let us consider briefly how knowledge of English Phonetics and *rigorous* and *long practice* in English speech can be given to all those who might one day become teachers, direct teachers in schools, colleges, universities and teacher training colleges, and even more widely influential indirect teachers in the media. If you do not believe me about the awful reality of speech in the audio-video media, just listen to one recent advertisement: it purports to sell a high speed easily portable internet attachment but ends up saying, "Speed! You can carry!" instead of saying, "Speed! You can carry!" And yet, as in Robert Browning's poem "Porphyria's Lover", God has not said a word, where God stands for English Teacher!

There can be no doubt that every teacher of language, *any* language, ought to strive to speak that language as well as possible. There is no point in quibbling about which standard he ought to acquire or practise. Any standard will do—if our colleagues command the full spectrum of speech in Caribbean speech, why, they can use that as a standard, as long as they acquire the power to be whatever they need to be in it; if they believe they can command South African English speech—and a most charmingly polite sounding dialect it is—why, let them speak in South African English. But to ride rough shod over the speech patterns of a language is the worst service one can perform to a medium that also happens to be one's subject of teaching, especially as that medium provides one's daily bread nowadays rather thickly buttered on both sides!

In very simple terms, teachers ought to put themselves through the beginners' course in phonetics and another in English speech. They should attend refresher courses specifically meant for this purpose, identify and practise from excellent varied and rich models of speech, make sure that for all intents and purposes and under normal circumstances at least they can speak a standard variety of English—very difficult to find in the Indian audio-video media today. By the way, a few decades ago it appeared that the leaders among audio journalists might serve as a model. Today they and their so-called experts speak varieties of English that are hardly credible when reported: a political-economic expert belonging to a party somewhat left of centre said only yesterday on a national television channel, with reference to a somewhat corpulent Marwadi on the discussion panel, "Look at Mr. Hiranandani's ooxing chicks!" And without the least exaggeration a Bengali professor of science said on a University level UGC programme in science a few years ago: "Take a shit of glass". Incidentally, such mistakes (which many television reporters pronounce as *mystics*!) occur by the many hundreds per minute in the television medium.

These are very far from being occasional errors or amusing curiosities, *variable* error being the norm now; indeed *different* errors appear on television channels everyday that vary freely according to reporters' linguistic background and their unfamiliarity with even the commonest of English expressions. So a dependable model will have to be found and acquired that contain no marked regional treasure trove of errors: for instance, in one corner of Indian people call a "phone" *fon* and a "job" *Job*; yet they pronounce the Biblical name Job as *Job*. In another part of India they pronounce "severe" as *sveer* and most Indians pronounce "sever" as *severe*, so the title of the Irish Murdoch novel becomes "The *Severed* Head" instead of *The Severed Head*! Yesterday indeed a Tamil student said that the English sonnet started with Surrey and *Yat*, meaning Wyatt. The poor fellow was merely imitating his teacher. Yes, the principle is the *same* in all aspects of language teaching: students will imitate whatever their teacher says, therefore if he says the more or less standard thing, so will his students.

But very few teachers can really request anyone to do anything by a change in tone, or scold anyone in appropriate tones; very few can express surprise without *saying* that they are surprised; no one can distinguish between a casual apology and a deeply felt apology in English without changing words.

From saying a routine "Good morning" to someone to saying "How are you?" to someone who has been rather ill recently, we need to manipulate English speech—which we mostly do not do, although it is most certainly part of what is called "communication". But such manipulation of speech occurs at every moment in English and all other human languages. And of course literary texts are littered with verbal renderings of the most innocent looking yet life-like words and phrases that are, consequently, altogether lost upon teachers and students alike. They cannot in speech distinguish between "There are twenty passengers on board" and "There are twenty onboard computers".

It is as though instead of possessing a live pet animal one is satisfied with the poorly preserved pelt of that animal. The simplest of important things in the speech of any language is to change the whole grammatical structure and the sense of a construction by a change in tone. Yet we cannot manage that in our utterance in English. This treatment of a language that becomes more important by the day and now especially in the verbal domain, such satisfaction with the meanest of minimalist objectives, gives the term *'alpa-santushta'* a very new negative meaning, indeed. If there is one category of people in India who must always want more like Oliver Twist; it is the category of second language teacher desiring constant empowerment in speech. And he must scrupulously do so in the interest of not merely the privileged high-fee paying student but also the underprivileged student.

What might be some of the situations in which a teacher and eventually a learner of English needs to exploit the power of speech? Meeting a student or a colleague in the corridor is one. Depending upon your relationship with him and your mood and your objective of the moment, you can say "Hallo", "Hallo, there!" and so on. You can say "How are you?" as a routine greeting. If you are pleased to see them, however, you must know how to say all these in an upbeat manner, for instance modifying the last item from routine to warm by stressing *are* and not *How*: "how *are* you?" Similarly, you can express surprise at finding them thereby saying "Hullo" on a different (falling-rising) tune as I just did, instead of the usual "Hullo". Notice that here the vocabulary has not changed one whit, nor the word order, nor punctuation as realized in speech or inscribed in writing. Yet a *very* different level of communication has occurred.

Imagine a habitually late student asking permission to enter your class late and you wish to say a *reluctant* yes. The routine response "Come in" would be uttered in scuh a case as a flat and uninterested *come in*. But suppose you wish to feign an ironic warmth, deliver a sarcastic barb, then you will change both your vocabulary and your tone, saying with pretend warmth: "Come on in, come in, come in", so that he feels shamed before his whole punctual class. And you might follow that up with "I *don't want* you co-ming *late* to my *class*!" Equally, if you are concerned about a student's health, you will not ask in routine tone "How are you feeling?" but use a tone and an extra stress on *feeling*: "How are you *FEEL*-ing?" that one differently uttered syllable communicating your concern.

Examples can be multiplied at will of how a little twist in speech changes meanings and attitudes and the whole tenor *and* substance of communication in *any* language. Only, in English that is done by means of appropriate word stresses and swapping sentence stresses around just a few basic tunes of intonation. But, of course, that is tied up with a sense of the rhythm of English, which is unlike the beautiful native rhythm of any Indian language I have heard. Simply, stresses are fundamental to English speech; get them right and half the battle is won; get them wrong and half the battle is lost; but next, rhythm comes from appropriate spacing and squeezing of stressed and unstressed or weak syllables. Consequently, get the stresses right, squeeze the right weak syllables and add the right mixture of musical tunes—that is all it takes to speak English effectively. Easier said than done? But naturally, like anything worth doing it is worth doing well. For instance, it is customary to say "thank you" for every little thing; that is English idiom. And you *may* think that being able to say those words in an unvarying flat tune always means you have acquired English speech. But remember that if someone gives you a book to hold under a small note you are writing, that is to say he does you a small favour, you do not say "thank you" in a flat tone (which will be very, *very* rude, indeed) but somewhat lightly with your voice rising at the end, "Thank you". And you definitely not say it as though they had done you a great favour like saving you from falling under a bus—in *those* circumstances you say "Thank you" with your voice *falling* heavily. The tone makes all the difference between acknowledging a small favour and acknowledging a great favour.

Ladies and gentlemen, I keep saying to anyone who will listen that for second language learners there is no substitute to reading and hearing literature, for in literature one meets all such and innumerable other situations and speech patterns appropriate to them. Second language teachers and learners meet so little of the *life* of a language that they ought to rely heavily upon its reflection in literature. And then they would meet language that otherwise one only meets in real life. This is so true that one can open any page of a narrative, for instance, and find there a good deal of useful speech idiom. Here is a random example:

> That evening he rang up Rosemary in her flat. She said, "Hullo, Wing Commander. How did your party go today?"
>
> "It went off very well," he said. "I think they were pleased with everything."
>
> "I thought they would be."
>
> "They are great people," he said. "I was really impressed."
>
> "Had you never met them before?"
>
> "No," he said. "I'd read about them in the papers, of course. But you can't believe all that stuff."
>
> "You can now," she said.

Now, this is a perfectly ordinary conversation in Nevil Shute's novel *In the Wet* (1953) about an Australian pilot meeting the

British Queen and her family. Yet it is chock full of the simplest and most effective tricks of speech that makes it the liveliest thing outside life. One not only can but must master how to speak, because without it one will only understand the lexical and grammatical meaning of the dialogue but neither its spirit nor its markers of living sense. Whether one meets literature in poetic form or in prose, whether in a comic story or in a play, it comes closest to living situations—Samuel Johnson probably had no idea in how very many senses his dictum was true, that literature holds a mirror up to nature or real life. Here is just one more sentence from George MacDonald Fraser's rollickingly funny *The General danced at Dawn* (1970), full of the most endearing Scottish accents, about why men from Glasgow were smaller: "They were extremely neat men, as Glaswegians usually are, quick, nervous, and deft as monkeys, but they were undoubtedly small. A century of life-of living, at any rate—in the hell's kitchen of industrial Glasgow, has cut the stature and the mighty physique of the Scotch-Irish people pitifully." One can dwell on the sense of the phrasing "life-of living, at any rate" for hours, it is so philosophically significant, and so eloquently delivered in speech, and yet it is only an *obiter dictum,* a passing remark, in the comic narrative. Undoubtedly when we read the literature of a language, we miss the core of the meaning of everything unless we can see it with our eyes and hear it with our ears!

Here are a couple of examples from poetry. You might meet this snatch in a little decorative anthology of verse about Songbirds:

> To hear the lark begin his flight,
> And singing startle the dull night;
> From his watch tower in the skies,
> Till the dappled dawn doth rise.

You will have to do a double-take in line 2, and work out its grammar in the mind, supplying the punctuation required, and read the line as "And singing, startle the dull night", even as you may be busy connecting the sound of "dappled dawn" with Gerard Manley Hopkins' "The Windhover".

> I caught this morning morning's minion, kingdom of daylight's dauphin, dapple-dawn—drawn Falcon, in his riding of the rolling level underneath him....

But you will certainly be surprised to learn that the upbeat sound of the verse about the lark comes *very* appropriately from John Milton's upbeat poem "L'Allegro" (ll. 41-44). Reading will constantly present one with examples of this kind as well as useful language in other verses such as this from Robert Louis Stevenson, as long as one is prepared to apply to them the rules and models learned in class:

> A birdie with a yellow bill
> Hopped upon the window sill,
> Cocked his shining eye and said:
> 'Ain't you 'shamed, you sleepy-head?'

You can always say the whole verse to your roommate in the hostel or to a child who is difficult to wake up! Your real command of the language will manifest itself in rendering even little humorous bits of a verse written for children's such as this:

> Call alligator long-mouth
> Call alligator saw-mouth
> Call alligator pushy-mouth
> Call alligator scissors-mouth
> Call alligator bumpy-bum
> Call alligator all those rude words....
> But
> Better wait
> Till you cross the river!

That such reading will provide you with an endless supply of examples to learn English speech is beyond a shred of doubt.

From such examples and nursery rhymes, which are ideal learning material in any language and especially in a second language, to what many of us consider a higher class of poetry is only a change of degree in demands made upon one's powers of speech. One can hear what one is capable of hearing, because in the hunt for meaning one goes to considerable lengths to exploit the verbal means available. From a colleague saying exasperatedly to repeated questioning about what went wrong with the department computer, "I don't know!", to a speech by Hamlet or King Lear, one travels a route by the same devices of speech. Equally, what one understands also depends heavily upon hearing the spoken rendering of language *even when one reads it with one's mouth closed.* Remember the testy retort in Shakespeare's *Hamlet* to Gertrude who says to her son that he seems sad: "Nay, not seems..."? And there is the incredibly effective opening scene of the play with its *initial* reversal of normal military routine and alternation between that reversal and the routine during the opening lines of Act I, scene i. They set the tone of the whole play:

> Barnardo: Who's there?
>
> Francisco: Nay, answer me. Stand and unfold yourself.
>
> Barnardo: Long live the king!
>
> Francisco: Barnardo?
>
> Barnardo: He.
>
> Francisco: You come most carefully upon your hour.
>
> Barnardo: 'Tis now struck twelve, get thee to bed Francisco.
>
> Francisco: For this relief much thanks, 'tis bitter cold and I am sick at heart....

Ladies and gentlemen, since I began exemplifying my ideas from the most mundane of utterances in English, allow me to conclude by reading out a few lines from *King Lear* which voice the old man's helplessness and a resurgent shadow of his erstwhile powerful self as effectively as any speech in drama in any language. Here in Act V, scene iii, he appears bearing the body of Cordelia in his arms:

> Howl, howl, howl! O, you are men of stones.
> Had I your tongue and eyes, I'ld use them so
> That heaven's vault should crack. She's gone for ever.
> I know when one is dead and when one lives.
> She's dead as earth. Lend me a looking glass.
> If that her breath will mist or stain the stone,
> Why then she lives.

2

Teaching the Phonetics of English: Case Studies

D. Murali Manohar

This paper tries to present the cases of teaching Phonetics of English at different levels and places. It also suggests how the English teachers ought to be knowledgeable about teaching them. Many of them ignore learning or taking phonetics seriously. Whether one implements phonetics in one's own life and in his/her day-to-day speech or not, nevertheless, being the student of English literature one must have the knowledge of it.

Introduction

Phonetics is considered to be a useless area to study by many teachers including university teachers. I have always wondered why many teachers try to bring in patriotism in the midst of teaching phonetics or using Received Pronunciation. They say I am proud of my Indian accent and I need not follow British accent. Why should I? Before any one claims: why he/she should learn phonetics, I would like to ask, do you have phonetics of English? When you had it in your syllabus, did you show interest? Did you ignore it due to your patriotism? No. It was uninteresting/difficult, therefore, you did not pay much attention. Are you not generalizing about it? Phonetics is like the English alphabet. Phonetics is part of the curriculum-from school to post graduation. How many teacher trainees and teachers are trained in phonetics of English and equipped enough to teach phonetics? Teaching the phonetics of English can be noisy, provided the teacher himself/herself is enthusiastic in teaching the students. The inspirer ought to be the phonetics teacher.

Objectives of Teaching Phonetics

- To listen and identify all speech sounds in English.
- To recognize all the English sounds with the help of a dictionary or of pronouncing dictionaries.
- To enable them to comprehend and speak English in any part of the world.
- To enable them to write any sound of English in a given context.
- To enable students—whether school, college or university students—to learn and apply phonetics in his/her academic life and life in general.

Review of the Situation

All English teachers ought to know phonetics. They study it but ignore or forget it. How many teachers choose to teach phonetics which is part of syllabus? According to Peter Mac Carthy:

> If pronunciation is to be taught, time must be found for it. And to neglect the manner of speaking a language—its pronunciation, that is—can only produce lop-sided course of language study—as lop-sided as if one were to neglect its spelling, or its grammar! (1967: 107)

Methodology

The method I approached for teaching phonetics was to use interactive sessions. I made each and every student repeat the sounds which I wrote on the blackboard. The students were initially very hesitant. However, I had to explain the importance of saying the sounds aloud. Shyness, fear and anxiety should be set aside. Initially they were not willing to open their mouth wide. They felt very shy in uttering the sounds. They made fun of the contortions I was indulged in. If the teacher himself/herself sheds shyness, superiority and unfriendliness, then the students also put these aside and participate in the sessions.

Case Study 1

I now present my experiences of teaching phonetics. I begin with my experiences of teaching students of Class VIII at Jawahar Navodaya Vidyalaya, Pabra, Dist. Hisar, Haryana State. This was their third year of English. I was appointed as Post Graduate Teacher in that Vidyalaya in November 1995. I found some aspects of phonetics in their English textbook. I went to Class VIII and asked whether they were taught those aspects. They said no. I started teaching them the vowels. I had drawn the vowel chart which they did not understand. I explained how the tongue has been approximated in the following diagram:

Vowel Chart

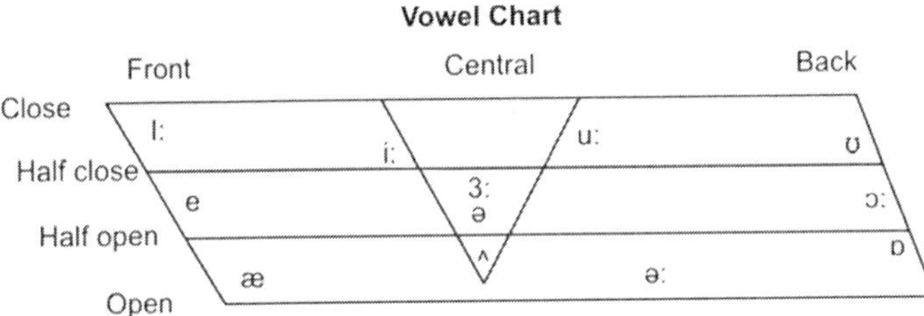

However, I took up each vowel and uttered it loudly. As I uttered each vowel, I asked them to observe my mouth and lips. When I uttered the first vowel /i:/ and second vowel /I/, I drew their attention to the position of my mouth which was un-rounded and that the length of the first vowel is long and the length of the second vowel is short. After explaining the theory part by drawing attention to it, I made them say the vowels aloud simultaneously. Why was it simultaneous? It would make them differentiate between the long and the short vowel. After explaining to them about the length and shape of the mouth, I had explained to them from where these sounds had been produced. By showing the chart I had told them the first vowel /i:/ is placed between close and half close and the tongue is neutral. For the first and second vowels there was a voice therefore they were voiced sounds. I also made a general statement that all vowels are voiced sounds. Vowels are generally voiced. Having explained the theory part I gave them some examples such as *eat* as in /I:t/, *sleep* as in /sli:p/ and for the second vowel I gave examples such as *hit* as in /hIt/ and tip as in /tIp/. After giving the examples they had to come up with a number of examples. I wrote all the examples that the children gave on the blackboard. If I had not done so, they would have been hurt, and the next time when I wanted their participation in the class, I would not have got it.

Evaluation

What was the result of this method? The result of this method was that the children enjoyed learning something that was previously not taught to them. I did not teach them from the examination point of view. Everything need not be looked at from the point of view of exams. Students also do not approach knowledge always from the exam point of view. In fact, topics such as phonetics should be taken up in class just before the board exams. This eases the tension of preparing for exams. Moreover, such a topic when taken up in class gives personal satisfaction to the teacher.

Case Study 2

I have already raised a question that how many of the teachers have knowledge of phonetics. I happened to come across a teacher in a teacher training college (Govt. B.Ed. college) who was exposed to phonetics in his B.Ed. but he was diffident in teaching to his own students who happened to be Teacher Trainees. I was on my summer vacation. I happened to see him and he had requested me to cover the topic of phonetics. I did it in two B.Ed. colleges in Kurnool.

Unlike in Vidyalaya, I had to teach both vowels and consonants. I had to teach two days in each college. The class strength was around two hundred students in each college. In both the colleges I used an over head projector for teaching vowels and consonants. I also used one of the students to draw diagrams of the mouth organs. I could only cover the topic from the examination point of view. How can any one teach all the aspects in two days? I had the satisfaction of knowing that I would be able to give some idea of the topic and that they would be able to answer some questions in the exam.

The methodology I adopted was mixture of lecture and interactive. I would have liked to use interactive method but I could not as the class consisted of 200 students. There was a little by way of questions; the rest was in the lecture method.

Evaluation

The lectures were not as satisfactory as it was with VIII class students due to the strength difference. Though overall output was satisfactory.

Case Study 3

I was asked to teach to Remedial Coaching Programme students who were weak in English. In fact it was a class of SC/ST students who wanted to improve their English and Spoken English. I taught them about the vowels in one class and they liked it very much. In fact, they wanted more and more classes. I sought feedback on phonetics and they said that they had not been taught the subject nor had heard the vowels in English earlier. I was very happy that I taught something new to them.

The methodology that I adopted was totally interactive as the strength was around 15 students. I made them utter the sounds all the vowels until they got the sounds right. I, in fact, had given them examples for all the vowels. The test was that if they could give around five examples of each vowel.

Evaluation

I was once again as happy as I was with the Class VIII students. The reason was that the students responded to the classes and they got some new learning through me. For any teacher, how much knowledge he has is not important, how much of knowledge he is able to impart to the students is more important.

Conclusion/Findings

All the students whether they are school children or plus two students or post graduate students or teacher trainees required the phonetics of English. Can we say that having knowledge of phonetics is very useful and all of them welcomed it and wanted more classes from me? Hence I teach phonetics whenever I get an opportunity. I don't see which level of students are interested. I am ever ready to teach even my colleagues who may want it. It is a demystified that phonetics is not important, Received Pronunciation is relevant or not, should we have Indian accent or British accent or American accent. What is important is awareness and reasonable knowledge to teach or to understand phonetics of English which is part and parcel of life of English students and teachers.

Work Cited

MacCarthy, Peter. "Pronunciation Teaching: Theory and Practice". *Selections of E.L.T.* Ed. E.R. Lee. London: OUP, 1967, pp. 106-17.

3

Validity and Utility of Spoken English

V. Prasad

Introduction

The Navodaya Vidyalaya System is a unique experiment and unparalleled in the annals of school education in India and elsewhere. Its thrust is on tapping the inherent talents of rural and deprived children by providing them opportunities to proceed at a faster pace, by making good quality education available to them, irrespective of their capacity to pay for it. Such education would enable students from rural areas to compete with their urban counterparts on an equal footing. The National Policy on Education-1986 envisaged the setting up of residential schools, to be called Jawahar Navodaya Vidyalayas that would bring out the best of rural talent. These vidyalayas are managed by an apex body called Navodaya Vidyalaya Samiti (NVS) headquartered at New Delhi along with its regional offices in various cities of this country.

Its growth and success has been phenomenal both in terms of the number of vidyalayas that have come up throughout the country and also in fulfilling the objectives with which it was started. We, Navodayans, can proudly say that we are one of the biggest success stories in the field of education.

Its Objectives

- To serve the objectives of excellence coupled with equity and social justice.

- To promote national integration by providing opportunities to talented children, largely rural, from different parts of the country, to live and learn together and develop their full potential.
- To provide good quality modern education, including a strong component of culture, inculcation of values, awareness of the environment, adventure activities and physical education.
- To ensure that all students of Navodaya Vidyalayas attain a reasonable level of competence in three languages as envisaged in the Three Language Formula.
- To serve, in each district, as focal point for improvement in quality of school education through sharing of experiences and facilities.

An NVS (Envious) Scenario

The success thought has to be taken with a pinch of salt because I as a teacher still envy other educational institutions especially in the field of English language. In my 18 years in NVS and having served as a teacher of ELT in the states of Rajasthan, Orissa, Maharashtra and Puducherry, the challenges students pose to my faculty *(the pun intended)* are immense and most often understated. It is a catch-22 situation where I have to make a hard choice between:

1. developing the overall competency of the student in the language by introducing methods where his formative (5, 6 or 7 years depending on when he started his education) exposure to English language are refined, redefined and remodeled to suit his/her immediate needs. This I call as a race against time syndrome, the motto being **the greatest good for the greatest number.**

OR

2. adopt the purist approach where I become a stickler for rules in how the language should be spoken and expressed with the proverbial RP Bible as my sole guide and taking my students through the exciting

labyrinth of phonetics, morphology, syntax, etc. etc. Past experiences have revealed that this excitement has often ended in excruciation.

The Problem

Jawahar Navodaya Vidyalayas, in spite of its unique entrance exams for selection of students to Class VI carries with it certain inherent drawbacks.

1. The entrance exams, I think, are designed more to check a child's IQ rather than his language competence. The rider being that he/she is capable of picking up the nuances of English language irrespective of what his previous knowledge is. Therein lies the crux of the problem because the heterogeneous nature of the students (there are too many variables) doesn't correspond with the homogenous nature of the syllabus which an English teacher has to deal with. The quagmire deepens when I take into account the sheer diverse magnitude of the students who enter into the portals of Navodaya.
2. The revised syllabus as per the National Curriculum Framework has thrown up more serious challenges to the English teachers in Jawahar Navodaya Vidyalayas. A student entering this vidyalaya in Class VI has a very poor exposure of English. Since the thrust is on the rural talented children, their deprived and diverse background, with many cases of first generation learners itself a challenge to the language teachers in bringing them at par with the emancipated urban school students pursuing their education in private and elite schools.
3. The word "talented", I feel, is a misnomer again. With due respect and regards to the sanctity of the exam and to the child entering Jawahar Navodaya Vidyalayas, I feel that the word has certain misplaced priorities, namely the areas where he is talented, and competency in English language,

barring a few, is definitely not one of the components.

4. My experience again within Navodaya throws up many interesting leads. Students entering into the portals in Hyderabad and Northern-eastern regions have a definite head start over their lesser brethren in other regions and again within the Hyderabad region a child entering a school in Karnataka/Kerala shows an innate appetite for English language than say a child in Puducherry. And again within Puducherry where I am presently posted students near to urban blocks or pockets have a better feel for the language than a child who comes from a typical rural pocket.
5. In this Navodayan vortex the natural inclination of a language teacher is to equip him with "the language" and not with its "intricacies and subtleties."

The Navodaya Variables

Before coming to the methodology, I would like to present an analysis of a typical Navodaya Vidyalaya. I term it as the 'Ten Commandments' over which unfortunately an English teacher has no or limited command!

1. Vagaries of the class in terms of language competency and this range from personal experience is too high for comfort.
2. Allocated time for English as a subject is not sufficient. The maximum time which a student gets where he is exposed purely in English is about 40 minutes to 1 hour.
3. Relating English to the child's mother tongue is also a source of heartburn. The almost transliteration way of learning English language where the child tries to frequently seek co-relatives from his mother tongue proves to be disastrous.
4. Inherent language factors cannot be ignored, namely syllabus completion, (the bane of our system is we tend to judge a child's competence through the

written part) testing him through the written means. The verbal part is often ignored by the students and here a language teacher has to inculcate in him the necessity of the communicative aspect of language.

5. Accumulated English language disability is also a matter of serious concern. Unlike Hindi which they learn from scratch, the students come with many inherent English language disabilities which are deep rooted, namely the handwriting, poor reading and writing and comprehending skills. As these problems have never been addressed, the student is somewhat bewildered when he enters into the Navodayas.
6. Bilingual hazard. Even an English language teacher has to accept this ground reality that he cannot be a purist and sometimes he has to bend his own rule book and use the native tongue especially in areas where interaction in English may not be adequate in putting a point across to the student. This is true of classes VI, VII and even in Class VIII.
7. Liaisoning with other subject teachers is also a major drawback because more often than not it is found that teachers of other subjects take frequent recourse to the mother tongue so that the classroom interaction becomes more viable. Subjects like Mathematics take frequent recourse to such regional input in the formative years of the child in Navodayas.
8. Exposure to other resources where he can pick up the nuances of English language. Though Navodayas have woken up to this important issue of supplementing the language exposure through various A-V aids but still getting hold of an excellent native model to augment this exposure has proved to be difficult. The RP or American accent proves a bit too hot to handle in a typical Navodayan classroom.
9. Selection criterion is a long drawn process where admissions in Class VI sometimes go on till the academic year is almost completed. An English

teacher has no say over purely government policies of preventing drop-outs, it may not be possible to start from scratch. Lateral entry students in Class IX and Class XI especially the latter are another impediment for the language teachers.

10. Variable X is the rural factor. The urban students' exposure to English language in terms of peer exchanges, the accessibility to an English environment, the parental background, the English base in the pre-primary and primary classes is unfortunately found missing among the children who enter into the Navodayas. The sorry state of affairs in government schools (most of the children in Navodaya Vidyalaya, Puducherry, come from there), as far as English language is concerned, adds to the discomfiture of a Navodaya English teacher.

I would like to quote two extracts on a very thought provoking article which I read recently in an *ELT* weekly on English Language Teaching in Rural Area by Tarun Patel. He says:

> When a child enters in school at primary level, he is taught English language as a subject not a language. Stress remains on formation of alphabets not on speaking or listening. To enhance vocabulary they are forced to reach a long list of words. When these learners enter at secondary level they are competent enough in writing and understanding English language but this is cramming based not on creativity.

He further adds:

> Over centralization of educational policies, academic inflexibility of the system not only stifle innovative and pragmatic deviation but also create a flow with the current, pacifistic resignation among resourceful and well motivated educator. Teachers have very little to say in designing the curriculum.... The only assessment that matters is the year end examination and students typically study for it by cramming

answers to likely questions.... Some students especially the ones from vernacular medium schools, insist that they find the study guides more useful on tests and exams than the classroom instructions or studying their textbooks.

The Common Problems

Some common problems which are an impediment to English language acquisition which I have seen in my children are:

1. *Wrong habit formations in pronunciation*

E.g. (a) The word /fʊ:d/ pronounced as /fʊd/

(b) The word /sed/ pronounced as /seid/

(c) The word /aʊə/ pronounced as /hʊəver/ (this is true for all sounds beginning with the silent "h.")

(d) The /l/ is always pronounced in all modals like /kuld/, /wuld/etc.

2. *Native tongue anomalies like*

E.g. (a) All /ɔ:/ and /ɒ/ sounds are pronounced as /ɑ:/ as in pot, caught, ball, call, talk, what, sorry, etc.

(b) Students really struggle with the /ɜ:/ sound as in /bɜ:d/, /ɜ:θ/, /wɜ:d/etc.

(c) They have problem with the sound /ʒ/ as in the words pleasure, treasure which are pronounced as /tresər/, /mesər/etc.

(d) The sound /ʊə/ as in poor, tour, etc. are pronounced as /pʊ:r/, tʊ:r/ respectively.

(e) The students have problem with the final consonant cluster especially the "ed" form of past tense, example /la:ft/ becomes la:fed/, /wɔ:k/ becomes /wa:ked/etc.

(f) The sound /r/ is always pronounced even in cases where it is silent as in /bɑ:/, /kɑ:/etc.

3. *Sentence problems*

(a) Reading problems, i.e. inability to identify tone groups and sense groups in a sentence.

(b) Inability to use the weak form of structured or functional words and so the speech or reading doesn't sound convincing.

(c) Direct translation from the native tongue, especially in interrogative sentences like, / ju: a:r gɔ:iŋ tu sku:l a:?/, /ju: a:r nɒt wel a:/.

(d) Lack of appropriate tones in different types of sentences, especially in exclamatory and interrogative sentences.

The Methodology

What should a language teacher do in such a scenario? My approach has been to give precedence to:

(a) develop his/her overall language skills, with special emphasis on the communicative aspect of language, which in the modern context is the buzz word.

(b) equip the child with a sufficient degree of language competence where his/her oral and written skill is not distorted to the extent that it becomes unintelligible to the hearer (native or foreign) or the reader.

(c) remove as far as possible the inherent dissimilarities in pronunciation and stress of words in English language which he/she has unfortunately acquired because of the stranglehold of her/his native tongue.

(d) the penultimate aim being to produce brilliant students of general English.

(e) the ultimate aim being to make him/her a purist, that is, special students of English (that is entirely vested in him!).

The Phonetic Angle

As the paper is on the Validity and Utility of Phonetics, I would deal specifically with the methodology I follow as far as listening, speaking and reading are concerned without emphasizing on the written aspect.

I. *At the entry level*

Most of the students who enter our vidyalaya in Class VI suffer English language disability in the areas of Listening, Speaking, Reading and Writing. Hence my first priority as an ELT teacher is to equip them with certain basic skills in all the four areas of the language. The normal methodology is:

(a) to have a **talent search** programme for these entry level students after they have spent a fortnight with us. The first two weeks are a sort of preparation for the students to wean them away from their parents and their home sickness. This talent search programme is to give adequate opportunity to these entry level students to showcase their talents and it also helps the teacher to have a proper idea of the talents in a child.

(b) to device a system of segregation during the "remedial classes" where suitable inputs are given to students depending upon the language acquisition they have; their reading and communicative skills besides their listening ability in English language. It is more of a "preparation," that is to evolve some sort of a common playing ground where the endeavour is to bring some sort of uniformity among the students with regard to English language.

(c) Remediation is done not by considering the students as weak or underachievers but to lead them gradually to an idea of what English language is all about. It is primarily to get the students and the teacher on the same wave length.

(d) Normally the text books are shunned initially and the emphasis is more on the following areas:

   (i) Listening to and reading simple stories, passages, jokes, quotes, etc. (Normally I start with Class IV text books.)

(ii) Framing simple sentences: Substitution tables based on simple structures. It is more of a drill aimed at making everyone utter a few lines in English.

(iii) Peer study is encouraged where students with a certain amount of language acquisition are put in charge of a group of students (not very large, about 5-7 in a group). These group leaders are given short specific language tasks, especially reading and speaking assignments. It has been found from experience that the results are very encouraging with the leaders and the members in that group participating with great interest.

II. *Typical classroom interaction*

A typical classroom interaction in the junior level follows the following pattern:

1. Model reading by the students, either from textbook or unseen passages followed by a few introductory questions on what the student understood.
2. Loud reading by the students without any interference by the teacher.
3. The words which are mispronounced are written on the blackboard and word drills are conducted with appropriate stress.
4. Sentence drills based on tone groups and sense groups are taken up and repeated by the students with appropriate stress and rhythm. Students learn to differentiate between the content words and the functional words and their respective pronunciation.
5. The weak forms of functional words are practised to develop a rhythm in their reading and speaking skills.
6. The new words learnt are used in other contexts or in other situations.
7. Five marks are allotted in every unit test to evaluate the listening and reading skills of the students in the form of dictation, spelling tests and reading a

particular paragraph randomly picked up from the allotted textual portions.

8. Two consecutive periods are set aside on a particular day of the week for reading stories other than that from the prescribed text. Immediate feedback is elicited before the student is given another book.
9. Audio-visual aids in the form of short dialogues and short stories are shown once in a fortnight.
10. Half an hour of English news on Indian channels (the vidyalaya has Tata Sky) is viewed by the children after their dinner.

III. *In higher classes*

The following activities normally form a part of English language instruction apart from the classroom instruction:

1. Conducting morning assembly.
2. Anchoring of morning assembly by students is done on all days in addition to various CCA programmes done throughout the academic year.
3. Conducting mock interviews, debates and reading reports form a part of the regular classroom interaction.
4. Extempore 5 minutes talk based on various topics prove quite a hit among the students.
5. One day in a week is set aside to discus editorials that appear in newspapers. (The *Hindu* should be thanked for supplying us their papers at a subsidized rate.)
6. Listening to English news in foreign channels, watching English movies.

IV. *Phonetics, stress and rhythm*

A candid remark I would like to make on this topic is that, even I as an English teacher may not be able to do full justice because I am also a product of the same environment in which my children are. Here I would like to quote a certain extract from a topic titled: "Role of English in India—Varities, Status and Functions",

> English in India is one of the most dominant languages widely spoken in our country. Its importance in our setting cannot be disputed. It has, indeed, added another voice to the Indian multilingual repertoire and is likely to shape the future of many bright Indians as they gain facility in the language. However, in its long sojourns in Indian soil it has "Indianized" itself, and is accepted as a variety in its own right. While there is no codified variety which we can call Standard Indian English, however a "neutral" variety has emerged which is largely devoid of regional interference and can be considered as a "spoken" norm. This is what I try to attempt with my children.

Come to the edge. We might fall. Come to the edge. It's too high! Come to the edge. And they came, and he pushed, and they flew (Ms. Deepa Shah *ELTECS-ISL* Digest, 10 Sep 2009 to 17 Sep 2009).

Conclusion

The validity and utility of phonetics in English language has been debated and discussed for a long time now. The opinions are quite pluralistic. I, as a teacher of ELT feel that its validity and utility have many dimensions and factors. The teacher or the tutor has to decide how far he should bring this element into his classroom interaction.

As far as school education is concerned, especially in schools like Jawahar Navodaya Vidyalayas, the utility and validity of phonetics has to have a middle approach. I have to definitely draw a line between what my children need from phonetics and what phonetics can give to my children.

I end on an optimistic quote with the extracts of a gentleman who I feel must have been a Navodayan.

> ...we are currently ahead in the software industry but there is no relationship between being fluent in English and being a good programmer. Those who

have talent in the computer-programming field would certainly be bright enough to learn necessary English within-a-year-or-so at graduate level, even if primary and secondary education was entirely in native languages." (Ajay Kulshreshtha, Ajay@Kulsh.com, California, USA)

References

Jones, Daniel. *Everyman's English Pronouncing Dictionary.*

Phonetics and Spoken English, CIEFL, Hyderabad.

Parrot, Wayne. *How To Present A Successful Seminar.*

English Language Teaching Strategies Used by Primary Teachers in One New Delhi, India School by Bonnie Piller, California State University.

Language Teaching Using a Language Lab by Sarang Lonkar.

ELT Weeklies.

Sharma, Parul. "Proficiency of English Teachers in Delhi Govt. Schools."

"Kyle Yamnitz" Webmaster@LessonPlansPage.com

ELTECS-ISL Digests.

E-lessons from.macmillaneducation.com

4

Challenges of Teaching English Phonetics in India and the Mother Tongue Influence: A Brief Study

Durga Prasad Dash

Introduction

The teaching and learning of sound and sound system in the area of second language learning presents some of the most difficult challenges to its learners. These problems become further challenging if the learners are at an advanced age. The demand of learning English has increased manifold. English Language is no more considered as a colonial language. Some hundred years ago, this was restricted only to five to seven million native speakers. During the era of colonization, it had spread many other countries in the world. Now we have more non-native speakers of English in the globe. It has become an international medium of communication. We have around 750 million speakers of English around the world (Braj 1996). It has become very essential for students to master the art of good English speaking whether they are students of Engineering, Medicine or Management. English language has penetrated into many new domains in the modern era.

The present paper makes a sincere attempt to discuss the challenges faced by learners in learning English Phonetics in India. Here the focus will be on some of the problems faced by Indian speakers due to Mother Tongue Influence while speaking English.

What is Mother Tongue Influence?

Mother Tongue Influence (MTI) is a speech-related problem among the speakers while learning a different language other than their native language. The problem is that the habits of mother tongue enter unconsciously into the new languages which ultimately make the speech incomprehensible to a lot of people. MTI is the influence of our mother tongue on our accent, basically while speaking a new language. We find this problem more in speaking and listening.

Most of the Indian learners of English normally start conscious practice of English Phonetics at an advanced stage. Whether they are the students of English medium school or the vernacular Medium, they don't have much exposure to standard British English. Their problem in learning English becomes more complicated because of the influence of their first language or mother tongue. At an advanced age they start learning English with a strong phonological base of their mother tongue. These habits of Mother Tongue always interfere in the learning of English. We call this type of Interference as Mother Tongue Influence (MTI) on English. In other words, we also call it as Native language Interference.

Different regional learners have different problems while learning English. That is why we cannot frame a standard Indian English Model for all like German English or French English. Different people from different parts of India speak different English in their own way. Thus we have Tamil English, Bengali English, Telugu English, and Kannada English and so on and so forth.

Problems in Pronunciation and Mother Tongue Influence

When we compare an Indian language like Hindi with English, we observe that the former is basically a phonetic language. English is a stress based language. Stress is very important in English speaking. Most of the Hindi words can be pronounced by depending on the written forms. This feature of Hindi is a strong contrast to English. We find many peculiarities, while comparing the number of vowels and consonants of different Indian languages with English sounds.

The problem becomes more complicated because we have different types of scripts and sounds in different Indian languages. This leads to several problems of pronunciation. One difficulty is distinguishing phonemes in words such as said / sad; par / paw; vet / wet, etc. Consonant clusters at the beginning or end of words are more than Hindi. This leads to errors in the pronunciation of words such as *straight (istraight), fly (flay), film (filam)*. Compared to English Hindi has weak but predictable word stress. Learners therefore have considerable difficulty with the irregular stress patterns of words such as *photograph / photographer*.

Similarly, if a South Indian and a North Indian are talking about making things 'simple', you might hear it as either "*simbl*" or "*simpal*". Or you could hear "*konstrukson*" (construction), "*bhaat*" (what), "*aadio*" (audio), "*brekphast*" (breakfast). These are the few symptoms of MTI.

The non-native learners face problem at different points while speaking English because they find problem in pronouncing certain vowel and consonant sounds of English. For instance, the central vowel /ə/, the back rounded vowel /ɒ/, and the consonants /f/, /v/, /θ/, /ð/, /tʃ/, /dʒ/ are mainly difficult. The sounds like /p/, /t/, /d/ are normally aspirated in stressed initial positions, which are ignored by the Indian speakers, mainly by Hindi speakers. Many Indian speakers don't distinguish between strong stressed and the weak accented syllables in English. This makes the rhythm of their English speech very unnatural and artificial.

The Phonology of English is greatly influenced by the phonological system of the first language of the learner. For example, we hear Indians use retroflex plosives **/t/** and **/d/** in place of alveolar plosives **/t/** and **/d/**, which happen in Standard English. When we hear regional speakers, we find many peculiar deviations in their English. For example:

- *Egg* /eg/ is pronounced as /jeg/ by most Tamilians.
- Like that most of the Telugu speakers say Zoo as /dʒu:/ instead of /zu:/. Similarly they also pronounce uncle as /ʌnkul/ instead of /ʌŋkl/.

- A Bihari speaker of English pronounces school as /isku:l/ and stamp as /istæmp/.
- Bengalis and Oriyas don't differentiate between /s/ and /ʃ/. They speak *'sip'* and *'ship'* alike. Similarly they don't make any distinction between the words *'sit'* and *'seat'* in their pronunciation. Here they have problem in short /ɪ / and long / pronunciation i: /.
- Malayalees say /p/ in *temple* as /b/ and /t/ in *canteen* as [d] and [k] in uncle as /g/.
- Hindi speakers have some of the following MTI in their English.
  - /e/ is replaced for /æ/ and /ei/ in their English speech. They pronounce *train* as /tren/.
  - /ɒ/, / ɑ:/ and /ɔ:/ are always confused by them.
  - /w/ and /v/ are always confused. So they speak "west" and "vest" alike.
  - /f/ and /p/ are confused and /p/ is always used for both.
  - The long vowels of English are spoken too short by Hindi speakers mainly in final positions.
- Like these many other speakers in India pronounce the middle double consonants letters by prolonging them unnecessary. For example, words like *upper, utter, summer, running* are pronounced with /pp/, /tt/, /mm/ and /mm/ for a single sound.

This type of Mother Tongue Influence in the speech of Indians makes their English confused even to fellow Indians.

Some Other Challenges

- The foundation of English learning of students is weak as they are not properly taught by proficient teachers.
- Majority of English teachers in India have no formal training to teach all the four components of a language namely Listening, Speaking, Reading and Writing to their students.

- We don't have uniform methodology to train our English teachers.
- Our syllabus is more examination-oriented than training-oriented.
- We have to establish good modern infrastructure in our schools, colleges and universities to produce proficient teachers, who can teach English language to the millions of students of this country.
- Most of the examination test the student's English knowledge by taking written tests. In most of the cases, we don't find any examination testing the ability of the students reading, speaking and listening elements.
- We don't have any quality training centers to train our English teachers except a few institutes like EFL University, TIME Group, etc.

Conclusion

In most of the Indian languages the pronunciation and spelling have one-to-one correspondence. It should also be remembered that English language doesn't have consistent correspondence between written and spoken forms. Therefore teaching English in its standard format is somewhat difficult. So, the learners must be trained about this difference between Indian languages and the English language.

We should train the students correct word accent, sentence stress, rhythm and intonation of Received Pronunciation (RP). This model of Pronunciation is followed in most of the institutes who train the students in British English. This kind of accent is normally used by the educated people of South-East England. BBC follows this model for its newsreaders. They have to practise consciously to control the pull of the mother tongue or first language while speaking English. They should make some model imitation to get this. We need to start Language Laboratory concept from school level.

The supra-segmental features of English must be learned from a competent trainer or an educated native speaker. Learners should listen to speakers of BBC and other British

News channels. A rigorous and continuous practice of pronunciation under a good trainer is required. It is very essential to teach correct English pronunciation consciously as the adult learners don't have the child's simplistic imitation.

References

Balasubramanian, T. *A Textbook of English Phonetics for Indian Students*. New Delhi: Macmillan, 1981.

Bhansal, R.K. and J.B. Harrison. *Spoken English*. New Delhi: Orient Longman Ltd., 2001.

Braj, B. Kachru. "Opening Borders with World Englishes: Theory in the Classroom". *On JALT 96: Crossing Borders. The Proceedings of the 23rd Annual JALT International Conference on Language Teaching/Learning*. Hiroshima (1996): 10-20.

Chengappa, Shyamala. "Bi/Multilingualism and Issues in Management of Communication Disorders with Emphasis on Indian Perspectives". *Language in India* 9: 8 August 2009.

Connor, J.D.O. *Better English Pronunciation*. New Delhi: Cambridge University Press, 2002.

Kansakar, T.R. *A Course in English Phonetics*. Chennai: Orient Longman Ltd., 1998.

5

Spoken English Institutes and their Relevance

Sharda Acharya and *Trishna Kar*

This paper is an endeavour to entrench and encapsulate the sole mode of global connection with the aide and succour of one tongue, i.e. English and how its propagation is processed and utilized. But before that, "Is it at all necessary to talk?" People can definitely be saved and unperturbed if they didn't have to talk at all. Taxi drivers are not as chatty as we often believe them to be. The ride from the airport to the train station may be in silence. Even if he is told where the passenger is going, he drives and reaches. The former looks at the meter, pays him and says thanks. While buying train ticket, the officer is approached and said, "One Way to Mizoram". He Says, "Four Fifty". Money is slipped into the slot; ticket is taken and the person moves on.

Flight attendants never said more than a few words and when serving drinks did not even bother to speak, as they simply arched their eyebrows as if to say, "What do you want?" Where then is the area of use?

These are minimal instances of speechless management of communication. But the globe can't afford to pause a second in its orbital phenomenon with one-sec and pause in communication. In other words, the interplay of thoughts and ideas have to be continuous to keep existence get going.

We are endowed by nature with capacities for assimilating speech. Each of us is a living testimony of this fact, for each of us has successfully acquired that form of our mother tongue with which we have been in contact. These capacities are not limited to the acquiring of our mother tongue, but are also available for one or more languages in addition. The young child possesses these capacities in an active state; consequently he picks up a second or a third language in the same manner as he does the first. The adult possesses these same capacities, but generally in a latent state; by disuse he has allowed them to lapse. If he wishes, he may re-educate these powers and raise them to the active state; he will then by this means become as capable as the child, of assimilating foreign languages. Those adults who have maintained these powers in an active state are said to have a gift for languages. The idea behind discussing it all is, to first of all realize that we should not get away with the excuse that we are incapable of learning a new language. Here, it is English.

When William Caxton set up his printing press in London (1477) the new hybrid language (Vernacular English mixed with country French and Scholarly Latin) became increasingly standardized and by 1611, when the Authorized (King James) Version of the Bible was published, the educated English of London had become the core of what is now called Standard English. By the time of Johnson's dictionary (1755) and the American Declaration of Independence (1776), English was international and recognizable as the language we use today. The Orthography of English was more or less established by 1650 and, in England in particular, a form of standard educated speech, known as Received Pronunciation (RP) spread from the major public schools in the 19th century. This accent was adopted in the early 20th century by the British Broadcasting Corporation (BBC) for its announcers and readers, and is variously known as RP, BBC English, Oxford English and the King's or Queen's English.

Generally, Standard English today does not depend on accent but rather on shared educational experience, mainly of the printed language. Present-day English is an immensely varied language, having absorbed material from many other tongues. It is spoken by more than 300 million native speakers, and between 400 and 800 million foreign users. It is the official language of air transport and shipping; the leading language of science, technology, computers and commerce; and a major medium of education, publishing and international negotiation. For this reason, scholars frequently refer to its latest phase as World English.

In our view, to speak of English as a World Language is simply another way of drawing attention to the fact that it is an arena where conflicting interests and ideologies are constantly at play. In its passage from a small dialect spoken by a few thousands of people in good old Albion to its present day status as the language. Saddam Hussain signed his treaty of surrender to the allied troops at the end of the first Gulf War. As an off-duty BBC Reporter, John Sampson was able to strike up a sprightly little conversation with a shoeshine boy in New Delhi's Connaught Circle, all that has really happened to English is that the power politics being played by those who use it for whatever reason, and in whatever capacity, has become far more complex, and, as noted already, far more visible. So we can understand that it is the attitude of the users, that determines the purpose or purposes for which they ultimately employ the language. A Japanese businessman might learn it to strike trade deals in Brazil. A Russian might learn it to do research in Berlin. An Indian might learn it to practice some profession or the other in Canada, USA and England. In Salman Rushdie's words "English, no longer an English language, now grows from many roots; and those whom it once colonized are carving out large territories within the language for themselves."

In many places such as Asia, Africa and South America, the ability to learn English will determine who will increase their living standards and who will remain in poverty. Careers in education have provided satisfying occupations for English graduates in the past and will continue to do so. However, the ability to handle language effectively and clearly is valuable in any occupation. Many companies have discovered early in the

21st century that they can cut their costs of production by sending their jobs overseas. The proper term for this is outsourcing, or offshoring. So, when we learn how to speak English, the opportunities are limitless.

Scaffolding this urge, a number of spoken English institutes have mushroomed in the country. We are summarily going to ponder over a few of them running in India which claim to be making difference to the learning class. To start with the British Council, it is the United Kingdom's leading cultural relations organization and India is their largest operation worldwide. In India, they operate as a division of the British High Commission and have offices in the four main metros as well as a network of nine libraries. Through their centres and programmes, they promote the diversity and creativity of British society and culture. They do this by helping people to appreciate its vibrancy. They operate in 110 countries around the world, running similar programmes to those over there. The British Council has recently launched a new speaking and listening course for Intermediate level students: *Keep Talking*. It includes public speaking skills, listening and questioning skills, group discussion skills, conversation skills, extempore skills, vocabulary and pronunciation. And for upper-intermediate level, the course is *Spoken English Skills*. Before students join it, they take a test and an interview and their teachers decide whether they are eligible to join these courses. If their level of English is not high enough they will recommend an *Enhance Your English* course at their level. The trainers at British Council follow the communicative approach making the lessons interactive. They select interesting materials and audio-visual aids to stimulate pupils' interest in a topic. The British Council has also been an aid in Corporate Training, which includes Recruitment Testing, Trainer Training, Courses for Employees, Professional Training Workshops (intercultural communication, presentation skills, power writing, speaking clearly, customer care, coaching skills, international English, report writing, team working, time management) and e-learning.

Next we move on to another Institute called IEFL, Institute of English and Foreign Languages. The aims of its course are to increase fluency in Spoken English; improve students' pronunciation; give intensive listening and comprehension practice; increase students' vocabulary; improve students' knowledge of grammar and phrases for conversation and discussion; give students self-confidence in understanding and using English. And for that they have divided the course into five categories:

- General Course
- Full-day Intensive Course
- Course for the Mature Students
- English for Executives
- Junior Holiday Course.

IEFLians claim students to be taught:

- to understand the spoken English which we hear in our day-to-day life.
- to speak English books, letters, newspapers.
- to read English books, letters, newspapers, etc.
- to write personal letters.
- finally, to think in English.

Hira Spoken English is a group having handled about 3000 students from various countries and also from different universities in the southern states, Delhi and Haryana in India. They have a unique strategy of running a class of only *six students* at a time. They feel six students make an ideal set to interact with the faculty and also among themselves in all aspects of listening, speaking, reading and writing, thus taking care of the students' complete satisfaction. They do not apply blackboard concept. They do not even provide course materials. Because they say, language is a communication skill, to be practised and a mind-game to be played. No matter how many books one reads on swimming or cycling, one should jump into the swimming pool and learn balancing afloat and then paddle. One should mount bicycle first and learn balancing and pedal. Similarly, one who wants to speak a language should soak in the language atmosphere and speak. They provide just that.

Veta, yet another, is the Asia's largest premier academy for teaching Spoken English, which has 250 centres across India with its international office in Singapore. Formerly known as Vivekananda Institute, its training centres are always abuzz with activity. The learning experience in Veta starts with a need analysis. They have seven different programmes namely:

- Veta Foundation English
- Veta Fluent English
- Veta Pro English
- Veta IELTS/TOEFL
- Veta Accent
- Veta English Holiday
- Veta Sure Shot

Russells, Speech Masters India, India Education, Mahan India are some other emerging Spoken English institutes which aim at serving the same purpose.

Getting employed in a good organization is increasingly being associated to job seeker's ability to speak fluent and correct English. Therefore Spoken English courses are gaining much popularity in every big and small town in India. English speaking skills are today of great value to anyone who wishes to be successful in this highly competitive world. Spoken English skills arc especially required if you are willing to work in transnational or multinational companies or international organizations. In fact, completion of Spoken English courses can always give an edge over others even in various domestic organizations. Fluency in English is in fact required in most other organizations. If one is working in a school or a college, he/she is always expected to set an example by being an effective communicator.

As English is the medium of instruction in many higher educational institutions, pursuing a Spoken English course can help him/her a lot in properly delivering your lectures with correct pronunciation. English speaking courses can also help us a lot in our day-to-day activities and improve inter-personal relations.

In India, English-speaking courses are much in demand as English is one of the mediums of instructions in most schools and colleges. As a result, institutions offering spoken English courses are mushrooming through the length and breadth of the country. Consequently one can today pursue various short-term English speaking courses, certificate courses, diploma courses and even post-graduate diploma courses. There won't be an iota of doubt that they shall be worth doing.

6

Phonetics—Demand in BPO, Corporate and Software Companies

Sreedevi G. Mahapatra

'Skill is for Living and Wisdom is for Life'

India being a colonial conglomerate for over 200 years, and only a part of the populace has been exposed to the English language, but to a large chunk of population—Communication in English to the extent of awareness, apart from the proficiency has been lacking owing to the very structure and educational system of our country. The English language teaching and understanding has been stratified between the institution and the states and the disparity and with wide choice to either to go for the vernacular or "English" is being opted by a few affluent and majority specializing for the native or the vernacular languages. Those who are talented but still prefer the vernacular languages as a matter of *path of least resistance*. Now, the need of the hour is to go for a standardized single language like *Euro* a single unit of currency for trade and commerce. Hence, it is desirable a single unit of language like currency which is best suited as "English". However, it may be reckoned that we are foreigners to the language as such owing to our colonial environment; it just takes some effort and practising in the language to master it.

Today we are living in a "global village". The global village does not have a night and day and it is uniform 24 hours system with the advent of *internet* and a unit language is desirable for transaction of the business and commerce and to reap the economic growth and well being of the country and the subjects.

People correspond with others from around the globe on a regular basis, products are bought and sold with increasing ease from all over the word and "real time" coverage of major news events is taken for granted. English plays a central role in this "globalization" and it has become the *de facto* language of choice for communication between the various peoples of the earth.

Many English speakers do not speak English as their first language. In fact, they often use English as a *lingua franca* in order to communicate with other people who also speak English as a foreign language. At this point students often wonder what kind of English they are learning. Are they learning English as it spoken in Britain? Or, are they learning English as it is spoken in the United States, or Australia? One of the most important questions is left out. Do all students really need to learn English as it is spoken in any one country? Would it not be better to strive towards global English? Let me put this into perspective. If a business person from China wants to close a deal with a business person from Germany, what difference does it make if they speak either the US or the UK English? In this situation, it does not matter whether they are familiar with the UK or the US idiomatic usage.

A more difficult problem is that of raising the awareness of native speakers. Native speakers tend to feel that if a person speaks their language they automatically understand the native speaker's culture and expectations. This is often known as "linguistic imperialism" and can have very negative effects on meaningful communication between two speakers of English who come from different cultural backgrounds. I think that the Internet is currently doing quite a bit to help sensitize native speakers to this problem.

Multinationals invest a surprising amount to teach basic English skills to a wide variety of employees. These learners vary in level from beginner to advanced level. They are working in entry-level to management positions. They all strive to improve their command of English, and are usually successful in their efforts. Unfortunately, after attaining a certain degree of fluency they invariably run into the same problem: Communicating with a native speaker! WHAT! What good is all this teaching if they have problems communicating with the people whose language they are supposedly learning?

This is often the case, as other non-native speakers tend not to use idiomatic language; and use a limited range of vocabulary. Their grammatical use is often more "bookish". Students who study English as a second or foreign language tend to communicate their ideas with few cultural references. One certainly wouldn't expect German and Japanese businessmen to use sporting idioms from the US culture to communicate their ideas about a sales campaign. Another important point is that non-native speakers are usually more patient with each other when it comes to variations in pronunciation. All of these factors work together to help non-native speakers have a relatively easy time when communicating with one another.

Native speakers' use of the language often reflects their own cultural bias. They bring standard idioms into play that—in their own environment—seem perfectly natural. They often prefer a highly idiomatic use of the language. Phrasal verbs and slang creep into their expressions. Take for example the issue of connected speech: "I've got to go to the bank" easily becomes "I gotta go to the bank". These minor issues quickly become overwhelming to non-native speakers who are used to standard forms. This, of course, does not mean that native speakers use English incorrectly and speak in dialects. It does however mean that native speakers tend to economize and use English which, especially in today's hyper-speed world, is constantly evolving in terms of vocabulary, collocation and idiomatic usage.

Practice with Pronunciation Using English is a stress-timed language and, as such, good pronunciation depends a lot on the ability to accent the correct words and successfully use intonation to make sure you are understood. Simply put, spoken English stresses the principal elements in a sentence-content words—and quickly glides over the less important words-function words. Nouns, principal verbs, adjectives and adverbs are all content words. Pronouns, articles, auxiliary verbs, prepositions, conjunctions are functional words and are pronounced quickly moving towards the more important words. This quality of quickly gliding over less important words is also known as 'connected speech'.

In a plain manner focusing on the 'correct' pronunciation of each word, much as some students do when trying to pronounce well. In the natural manner with content words being stressed and function words receiving little stress.

Speech communication is considered as an interpersonal and practical activity. This is a humanistic way of involving people relating to people. Its functional role involves goals and means of being effective in communication. Through communication we build kinship with others, build a base for cooperative relationship and understanding. So in order to communicate it is necessary to know something of what others value, their outlooks on life, their interests and inclinations. There are about three to four thousand languages in active use today. Languages are like people—appear similar but have great variety. So how do we penetrate the differences to arrive at the sameness underneath?

According to the linguist Dwight Bollinger, "the science of phonetics, whose domain is the sounds of speech, is to linguistics what numismatics is to finance: it makes no difference to a financial transaction what alloys are used in a coin, and it makes no difference to the brain what bits of substance are used as triggers for language—they could be pebbles graded for colour or size, or, if we had a dog's olfactory sense, a scheme of discriminated smells. The choice of sound is part of our pre-human heritage, probably for good. We do not have to look at or touch the signaler to catch the signal, and we do not depend on wind direction as with smell—nor, as with smell, are we unable to turn it off once it is emitted". Thus if we learn a language we must learn to produce sounds which are understood by others.

Oral and written language shares many common features: the same vocabulary, the same grammar and syntax, and similar purposes. However, to construct meaning from the printed language (reading) and to use printed language to convey a message (writing), students must be able to recognize in print the language that they use orally (Mason, Herman, & Au, 1991). The difference between knowing the keys of a piano versus playing the instrument:

- As any student of English can attest, written English is only an approximate representation of the spoken language. Phonetic transcription, in contrast, is an exact representation, without any ambiguity, redundancy, or omission. In a phonetic transcription, every symbol stands for one sound and one sound only. There are no "silent letters," nor are there any spoken sounds that are not represented in the transcription.
- A phonetic transcription can be used prescriptively, to show students how a given word or phrase should be pronounced. The transcription can represent a precise, standard pronunciation, independent of the individual or regional accent of any teacher or audio recording. It thus allows students to see the correct pronunciation of an English word of phrase without the confusing influence of any anomalies in an instructor's speech, and provides a reliable, ideal model towards which students can work in their pronunciation, independently of the speech of any human instructor. Dictionaries use phonetic transcription in this way to indicate the "standard" pronunciation of words.
- A phonetic transcription can be used diagnostically, to record and analyze the speech of students. A student can often better understand his errors in pronunciation if he sees them laid out in static visual form. One might say that a picture is worth a

thousand words, with transcription being the picture, and words being the spoken language. Students can compare transcriptions of their own speech to that of "model" speech and see and correct their mistakes.

- Phonetic transcription is useful to show the significant differences between the pronunciation of isolated words in a dictionary and the actual pronunciation of those same words when they are grouped together in connected speech. Students can see why connected speech is much difficult to understand when they are shown the modifications in pronunciation that occur in such speech, and they can learn what modifications to expect and how to recognize them. They can also adopt a more natural-sounding speech themselves by noting the "standard" changes that occur in connected speech and emulating these themselves.

Moreover, in medical transcription lack of phonetics knowledge will lead to catastrophe where diagnosis to prescription depends on the sound and spelling.

This brings us to the interesting conjunction of language and business opportunities which has given rise to a phenomenal growth of the Information Technology and Enabled Services (ITES) sector.

According to a report, Indian Companies maintained their share of 45 per cent in the global BPO market and more than 65 per cent in the IT Software Outsourcing market till 2010, even as the combined market is estimated to have grown 10-fold from $30 billion to nearby $300 billion. India Information Technology Consulting, Offshore Software Development, Research & Development and other BPO sectors have seen almost 10 times growth, uptil $166.5 billion. Software Outsourcing and BPO services have approximately 2.3 million people, besides providing indirect employment to another 6.5 million workers, according to the report by 2010.

The growth of the IT-BPO sector has been synonymous with India's rise to prominence on the global map especially in the last two decades. The industry gainfully employs over 2.23 million people, leading to increased tax collections, enhanced consumer spending and more inclusive growth. Additionally, the industry has today become a growth engine for the economy making substantial contributions to GDP, generating foreign exchange through exports, and leading to the establishment of a host of supporting industries. Every IT industry has led to the creation of 3.6 million additional jobs in related sectors to achieve the vision of a "young and resilient" India and reiterating the viability of India's fundamental value proposition.

Clearly, global sourcing is a 'win-win' proposition; and has been emphatically demonstrated in the significant gains achieved by developed as well as developing countries that have participated in the growth of IT and Communication related business.

During the recent years, the sector maintained its double digit growth rate and has been a net hirer. This growth has been fueled by increasing diversification in the geographic base and industry verticals, and adaptation in the service offerings portfolio. Consequently, India has retained its leadership position in the global sourcing market.

Strong fundamentals, a robust enabling environment, and enhanced value delivery capability are the hallmarks of the Indian IT-BPO industry. India's fundamental advantages—abundant talent and cost—are sustainable over the long term. With over half the population of India aged less than 25 years, India's young demographic profile is a unique and an inherent advantage. This, complemented by a vast network of academic infrastructure and the legacy effects of British colonization has contributed to an unmatched mix and scale of educated, English-speaking talent, where over 3.5 million graduates and postgraduates are added annually to the talent base, no other country offers a similar mix and scale of human resources.

While some gaps in talent suitability exist, they are being addressed through strong provider-level initiatives and industry-led programmes. India enjoys a cost advantage of around 60-70 per cent as compared to source markets.

Additional productivity improvements and the development of their 2/3 cities as future delivery centres, is expected to enhance India's cost competitiveness.

India's IT and business process outsourcing (BPO) services industry could be bringing in $60 billion by the year 2010, growing at nearly 25% a year. India's software and services exports were $17.2 billion in the fiscal year that ended in March 31, 2005, up by 34.5% from the previous year, according to the National Association of Software and Service Companies (Nasscom) in Delhi.

The fact is that India's Offshore Software Outsourcing industries had grown three times more from $4 billion in 2000 to $12.8 billion in 2004. While services exports grew 60% from $16 billion in 2000 to $25 billion in 2004. "The upcoming five years will tell a story of the huge increase in the global Software Outsourcing potential. Market share of India's in total will remain steady and the country will capture a significant proportion of the total market opportunity in world. Software outsourcing companies need to stay ahead of competition from low-cost destinations like South Africa, China and east European countries which are their major competitors in the world of software outsourcing.

Indian companies had cornered a very small slice of the Software Outsourcing cake in several verticals. Faster and healthy innovation could spur further growth in Software Outsourcing Development India by effective professionals. The increase in the global market potential for the BPO sector would be driven largely by finance and accounting and traditional industries, the IT industry would grow on the back of newer technologies and R&D is the fact.

For instance, the penetration in the banking services business was estimated at 10 per cent, while only 9 per cent of the potential auto manufacturing business had been tapped. This gives Indian companies a vast opportunity to grow in these sectors as well.

Despite the difficulty in managing international relationships, workflows and expectations, companies today are looking for partners in India not just for piecemeal development work, but for strategic business projects which are valuable to them. Whether it's taking over a full product line or building half of an entirely new product, Offshore Software Outsourcing Development partners are becoming intrinsically engaged in India.

NASSCOM (the premier trade body and the chamber of commerce for the IT and BPO industry) has, on behalf of the industry, led the development of a comprehensive skill assessment and certification programme for entry-level talent and executives (low, middle-level management) and is organising an image enhancement programme to build greater awareness about the career opportunities in the BPO segment. The industry is also working with the University Grants Commission and the All India Council for Technical Education, to encourage and facilitate greater industry interaction, thus helping them share relevant feedback, stay updated on developments in the industry and giving them an opportunity to incorporate positive changes to their curriculum and pedagogy. Further, there is a proposal that a chain of 'finishing schools' be set-up, to supplement the graduate education attained by the next layer of candidates—considered unsuitable for direct employment in the IT sector.

India's core proposition of talent, quality, security and cost advantage would be inconsequential without the rapid growth in availability of high quality telecommunication connectivity across the country. Over a span of little over a decade, the Indian telecom market has evolved from a public sector monopoly to thriving free-market competition. Carefully crafted policy has helped drive a balanced agenda for the sector by influencing a decline in pricing and increased affordability on one hand and increasing access penetration and usage on the other, resulting in strong growth. The IT-BPO sector has been a key beneficiary, with the cost of international connectivity declining rapidly and service level quality improving significantly.

The globalization marathon has not only enabled a developing country like India to grow, but has also opened up numerous doors to success and career development. As the

BPO industry evolves, training and development stands out as a domain to identify, polish, groom and promote talent through people management skills. A large chunk of training resources in any BPO are constituted by voice and accent trainers.

Voice and accent training is one of the most popular training programmes in the BPO industry. It is designed keeping in mind the diversified globalised culture and the need of business outsourcing—the speech skills of Indian BPO employees are groomed and refined and they are taught how to improve their overall English conversational skills to meet international standards.

Voice and accent training enables the BPO industry to step forward and introduce the concept of American/British accent versus the Indian accent. The way an American speaks is different from the way an Indian speaks.

Voice and accent training imparts the basic concepts of the English alphabet and its corresponding letters, which further represent their respective sounds, and thereby improves overall conversational skills. A native English speaker uses vertical lip and jaw movement while speaking; on the other hand, an Indian uses horizontal lip and jaw movement while speaking.

This small difference affects the overall speech clarity and the ability to pronounce a word correctly.

Besides incorrect mouth or jaw movements, several other factors like the rate of speech, pronunciation, grammar and MTI (mother tongue influence of any native language over English) are major bottlenecks for an individual to overcome while he/she goes through voice and accent training.

Voice and accent training isn't just about making a fancy speech in English or demonstrating the accent of a native English speaker; the job of a voice and accent trainer is to train and groom people, who are not only different from others but also represent different cultural backgrounds and language dialects.

People who already know how to speak in English, however, miss out on the small aspects of the language, as small as the Hindi to English translations of their own ideas and the fact that Hindi is a phonetic language, whereas English is not.

Thus I feel that verbal communication is the front runner of written communication and there is a need for teaching sentence stress, falling tone or rising tone since the Asian languages have no such tone patterns. Phonetically, the Hindi language is spoken the way it is written and written the way it is spoken. On the other hand, the English language is not spoken the way it is written, nor written the way it is spoken. I would like to quote Mangesh V. Nadkarni's article titled "English as Global Language" wherein he says "There are enough indications that English as a Global language is gaining recognition as a special phenomenon. Thus, for example we have journals like *World Englishes* and *English—World Wide*, and books such as *English as a World Language, English Around the World* and *English in the World* devoted entirely to the study of Global English; all this is indicative of the fact that Global English is being recognized as a field of study of its own right. And yet it seems to me that we have been tardy in taking the next step, which is that of recognizing that the new phenomenon requires theoretical perspective of its own."

In longer-term business partnerships depend upon relationship-building and relationship-management. To achieve this, cultural and linguistic knowledge of the target country are essential. At the school level care is being taken of the written and spoken English but unfortunately in professional colleges and degree colleges where the need to train the students for a specialized global English is being ignored. There is immediate need to restructure the curriculum and a need for establishing International Institutes which would take care of Advanced Spoken Skills which have universal acceptability to suit the demands of the job markets. Develop and support programmes to raise awareness of the importance of language skill. Improve Business-Education links in relation to languages. Identify and disseminate models of successful collaboration between business and education especially, but not exclusively, directed towards the promotion of language skills.

Improve the articulation between European/national/regional/local language policies and the needs of business. Last but not least, in matters of business, it's the head that rules. And going by this practical approach India should emerge the winner. But for now, the jury is still out and the decision could go either way.

That brings us again to the important question—the role of language and phonetics. If with our intelligence we could master English, would it be difficult for us to master French, German, Italian or even Japanese? The road ahead lies in our ability to think out of the box and introduce appropriate incentives at the industry level as well as in the education system to provide for alternatives to English to retain our eminent position in the Software and BPO industries. If phonetics is the important piece of the jigsaw puzzle to solve the structure of the language once understood and mastered the benefits are enormous for the personal development and for unified thinking with the other parts of the world.

References

Atkielski, Anthony. "Using Phonetic Transcription in Class". Rev. 3. Dec. 2005.

Central Institute of English: The Sound System of Indian English, Monograph No. 7. Hyderabad: Central Institute of English and Foreign Languages, 1972.

English as a Global Language (second edition) by David Crystal.

English Language as Global Language by Mangesh V. Nadkarni.

Jepersen, Otta, "What is the use of Phonetics?" *Educational Review*, February, 1910.

NASSCOM Annual Reports 2006 & 2007.

The Economics of English by Indian columnist, Sucheta Dalal.

7

Phonetic Features of English Spoken by Indonesian: A Systemic Functional Orientation

Susanto

ABSTRACT

Phonetic features can be acoustically characterized by the concurrence of particular cues. They are not indivisible in the sense that they are indicated by a number of acoustic properties that are time varying, relative and not graded (i.e. not representing one particular value, but a continuum of values). The paper, then, aims to present an investigation of the phonetic features of English spoken by Indonesian.[1] Following the development of systemic functional orientation on phonetics (Halliday & Greaves, 2008), the paper attempts to demonstrate the value of system network and the notion of rank in positioning phonetics in the language dimension taking the object of investigation as a case study focusing on one target phonetic feature, i.e. place of articulation within nasals (Matthiessen, 1987; cf. Matthiessen, 2007).

1. Introduction

1. Indonesian people (later called Indonesian) are permanent residents of the Republic of Indonesia. The national language of the country is Indonesian language which is used basically as the *lingua franca* in the country. Out of the national language, it is reported that there are 726 regional languages spoken across the country.

Phonetic features which can be characterized by the acoustic cues differ with respect to their perceptibility. Acoustic properties can indicate the phonetic feature so that it is not indivisible. The properties as noted are time varying, relative and not graded (i.e. not representing one particular value, but a continuum of values). An investigation of the phonetic features of English spoken by Indonesian, then, is done as a case study.[2] Following the development of systemic functional orientation on phonetics, it is primarily to demonstrate the value of system network and the notion of rank in positioning phonetics in the language dimension by taking the object of investigation focusing on one target phonetic feature, i.e. place of articulation within nasals.

The paper is organized as follows: Section 2 provides a description of the phonetic features of consonants for their manners of articulation, voicing and places of articulation. Section 3 introduces the system network and rank in systemic functional framework. Section 4 describes the method employed in the investigation. Section 5 discusses the results of the phonetic analysis of the findings and the value of system network and the notion of rank in positioning phonetics in the language dimension.

2. Phonetic Features

It is well-known that there are basically three target phonetic features, i.e. manner of articulation (the way how the air stream is obstructed), voicing (vibration of the vocal cords) and place of articulation (the place where the air stream is most obstructed) and it is found that they contrast within and between consonants whether they belong to plosives, fricatives or nasals. The three features are all characterized by particular acoustic cues or complex combination of different cues indicating their occurrence.

---

2. All data used in this study were recorded from the writer's consultants; i.e. Indonesian students at EFL University, Hyderabad. Special thanks to them who were kind enough to lend their voices to this study.

A Two-Day National Seminar on Phonetics and Spoken English, 30-31 October 2009 at Department of English, University of Hyderabad, Hyderabad, India.

In manner of articulation, plosives are produced by blocking off the oral cavity as well as the nasal cavity by raising the velum for the air stream. Releasing the occlusion in the oral cavity results in the characteristic burst of sound when the air stream backed-up in the oral cavity can flow again. Fricatives are produced by squeezing air through a narrow constriction at some point in the oral cavity resulting in seemingly random, higher-pitched noise, differing in intensity and diffusion over frequency ranges. And nasals are produced by blocking off the oral cavity for the air stream and lowering the velum so that air can escape through the nose.

In voicing, acoustically it is context-dependent. But basically, it distinguishes between voiced and voiceless plosives and fricatives. It is not distinctive for nasals since air can stream unhampered through the nasal cavity.[3] For plosives and fricatives, an obstacle at some point in the oral cavity hampers the air stream. It results in an accumulation of air in the oral cavity which increases the air pressure. If the air pressure in the oral cavity approximates to the sub-glottal pressure, it will be voiced.[4] When airflow lapses below a certain level, it will be voiceless because vocal cords stop vibrating.

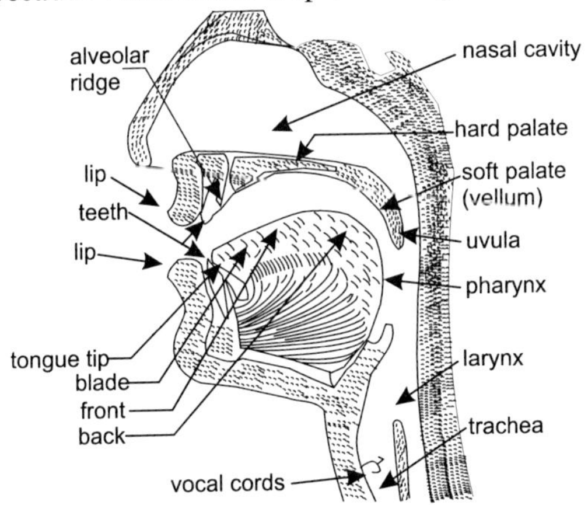

Fig. 1: Articulators in Vocal Tract

3. It results in evading the application of, what is called, Aerodynamic Voicing Constraint (AVC) which according to that voicing requires two basic characteristics, i.e. the vocal cords must be appropriately tense and abducted and air must flow through the vocal cords (see Ohala, 1997).
4. This condition infringes upon one basic requirement of the AVC, i.e. the airflow through the vocal cords.

In place of articulation, plosives have two context—dependently acoustic cues, i.e. the burst frequencies associated with the stop release and the formant transitions. The efficacy of the burst is influenced by the subsequent vowel. For fricatives, the cues are frequency spectra and formant transitions. A concentration of energy in the higher energy frequency range characterizes posterior fricatives. For nasals, the acoustic cues to the place of articulation are determined in the oral cavity. The location of the occlusion in the oral cavity determines the particular oral resonance. Formant transitions, then, are salient cues.

3. System Network and Rank

In looking at a dimension in which a language is organized in such a way—in context—that it brings the sense of carrying characteristics as semiotic system, the notion of 'stratification' is important to consider in the perspective of Systemic Functional Linguistics. The stratification is designed to model the organization of language in context as a number of ordered subsystems; i.e. context, semantics, lexicogrammar, phonology and phonetics (Matthiessen 2007).

The stratification covers comprehensively the range from meaning in context (i.e. context of culture and context of situation) to the manifestation of meaning in sound (i.e. sound materialized in the human body and in sound waves). System, then, develops within the stratification as the central category for representing potential organization at any stratum whether starting from phonetics or from context into system networks considering the related entry. In the modeling of a given stratum, the dimension of rank is taken into account. It reflects a hierarchy of units for the basic realization pattern. Having the notations of rank and system network in stratification, it can be comprehended how the sound acts 'as the resource with which the meanings of language are constructed' (Halliday & William S. Greaves 2008: 11).

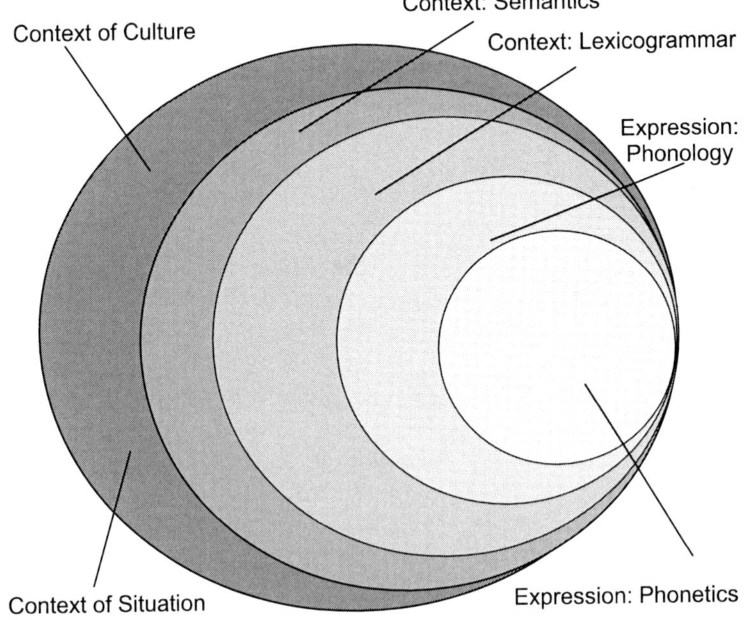

Fig. 2: Stratification

Source: Halliday & Matthiessen 2004: 25.

4. Method

Eight adults of Indonesian speakers of English were recorded for the investigation. Data was gathered by asking them to do two things, i.e. to elicit English words containing nasals /m/, /n/ and /ŋ/ and to narrate their experience in English. Subjects were directly recorded onto Sony IC Recorder ICD-PX720. The recordings were then transferred into a Fujitsu laptop computer using Sony Digital Voice Editor (ver. 3.2.00) and then analyzed using PRAAT program.

5. Discussion

In this section, firstly, results are presented in spectrograms for showing the spectral characteristics. The movement of formants, then, is traced to give the acoustic information about the place of articulation of the nasals. Based on the description, the system network, then, is built and the rank is created.

5.1 *Spectral Characteristics of /m/, /n/ and /ŋ/*

Nasals may not be easy to spot on spectrograms when the setting of bandwidth is not appropriate. In this case, the window length of the displayed spectrograms is 0.005 second so that the bandwidth is 200 Hz; i.e. 1/0.005 sec. The view range is from 0 to 5000 Hz and the dynamic range is 20 dB.

The spectrograms of *simmer, sinner* and *singer* respectively are given in figures 3, 4 and 5. The figures show that /m/, /n/ and /ŋ/ have a bar indicating energy near the base line at around 300 Hz. Also, there is some energy present in the 2000-3000 Hz region.

Observing the faint formants in the region of 1000-2000 Hz, it corresponds to a resonance of the body of air which is behind the closure. The formant of /m/ in *simmer* which is about 1200 Hz is lower than one of /n/ in *sinner* which is about 1600 Hz. And the faint formant of /ŋ/ in *singer* is the highest, i.e. about 1800 Hz. Hence, this can be used to distinguish the place of articulation of nasals. In labial nasal, the closure is formed at the lips which results in the large size of the body of air. In alveolar nasal, it is formed with the tongue blade at the alveolar ridge. It brings the narrower size of the body of air. Then, in velar nasal, it is formed by raising the tongue body to make contact with the soft palate (vellum) with consequence that the oral closure is very short. It is, then, noted that there is an increase of frequency when the closure moves back because the size of the body of air decreases.

Another way distinguishing the place of articulation within nasals is by observing the movement of the formants in the surrounding sounds. From the spectrograms above, it can be noticed that F2 and F3 of /i/ fall before bilabial nasal, are level before alveolar nasal and rise before velar nasal. The movement is the consequence of different formants in vowel /i/ and the nasal. It is observed that from labial to velar nasals, the frequency increases in the vocal tract. Hence, the falling movement of F2 and F3 of /i/ occurs before /m/ and the rising one before /ŋ/. The level movement of F2 and F3 of /i/ before /n/ is presumably caused by the approximately same frequency of them.

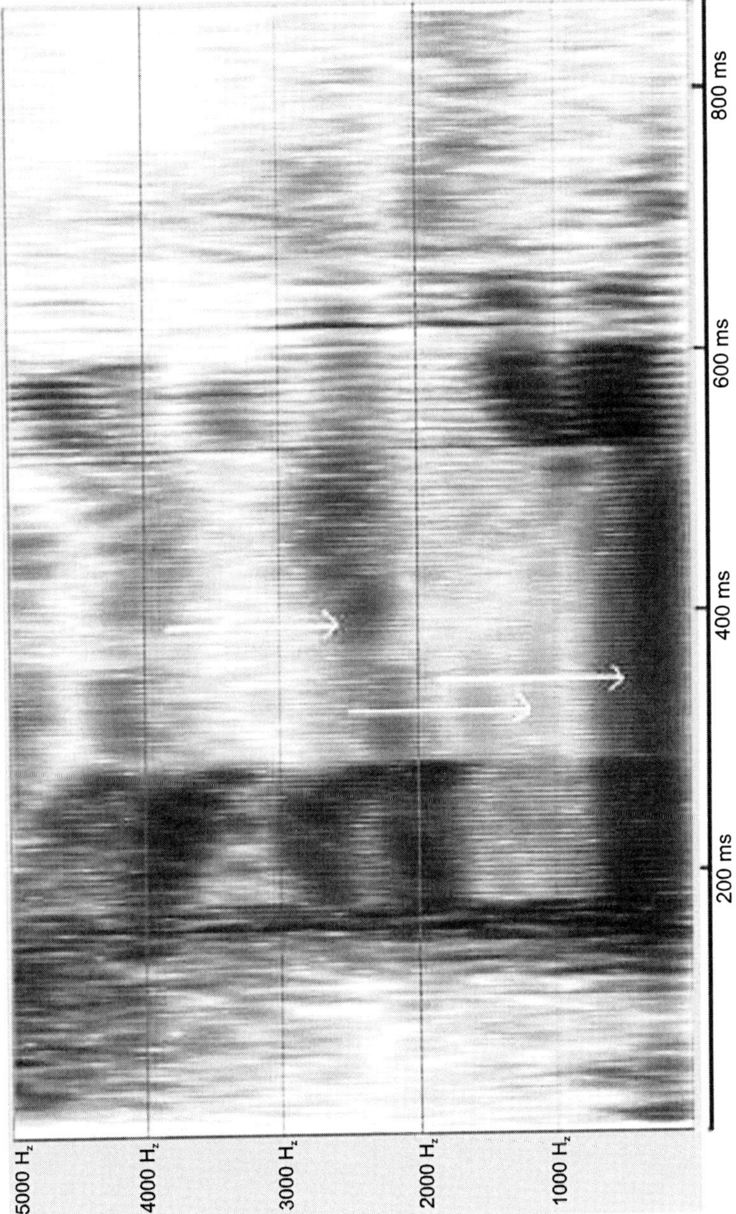

Fig. 3: The spectrogram of simmer

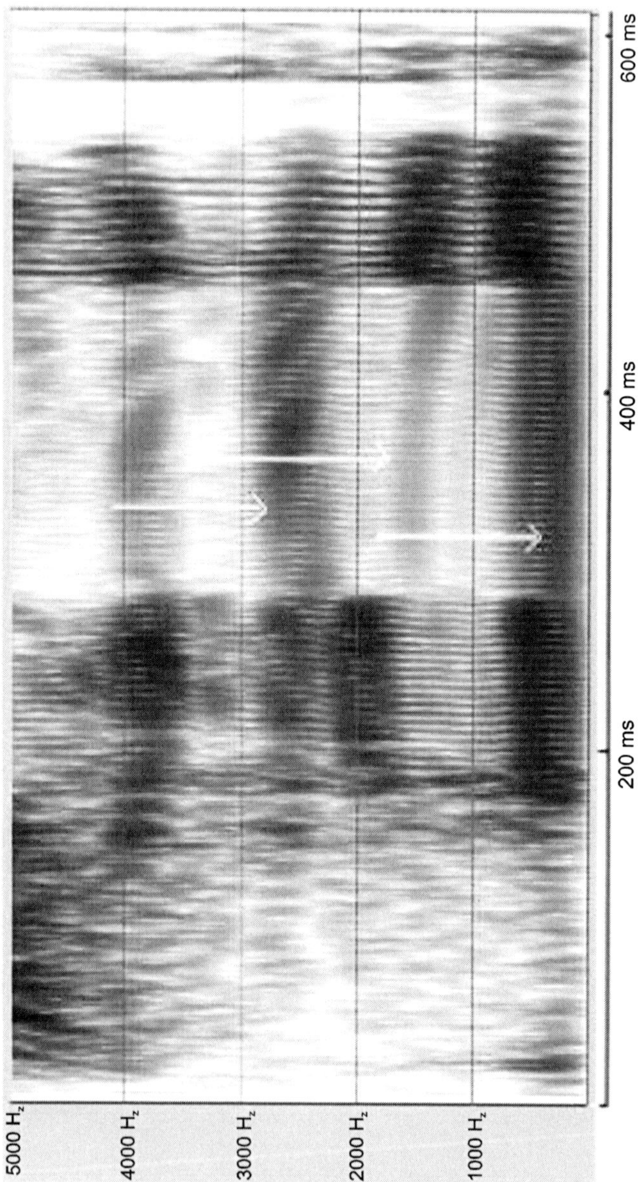

Fig. 4: The spectrogram of sinner

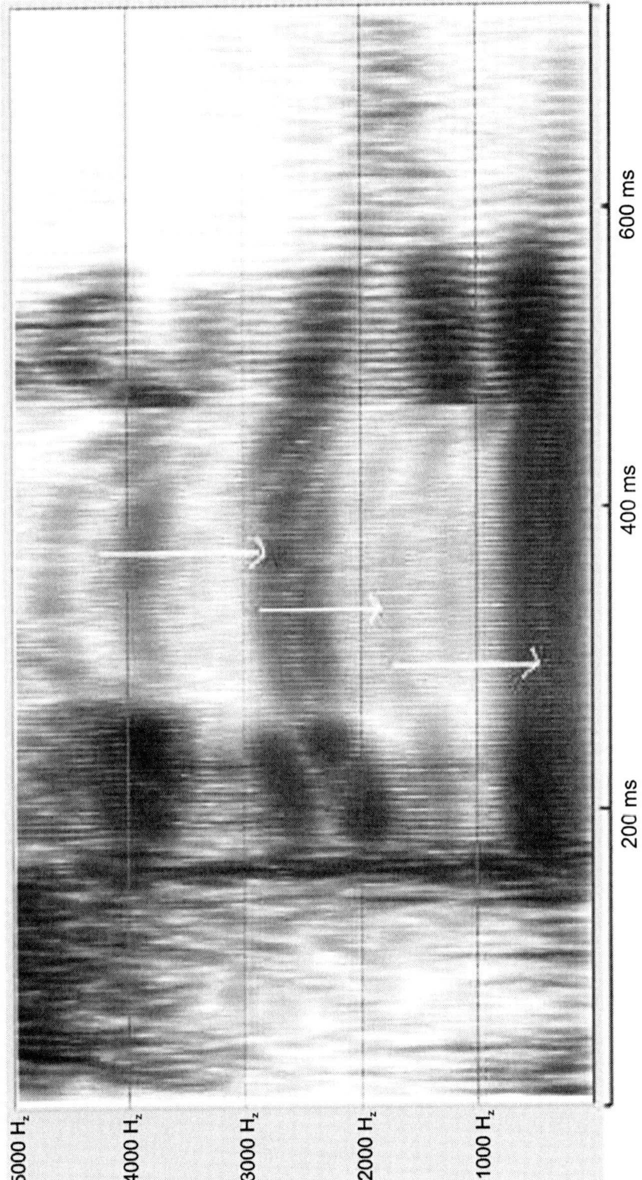

Fig. 5: The spectrogram of singer

5.2 *System Network of Nasals*

Matthiessen (1987) has drawn a system network for organizing the phonetic resources which is useful cross-linguistically as reproduced in figure 6 below.

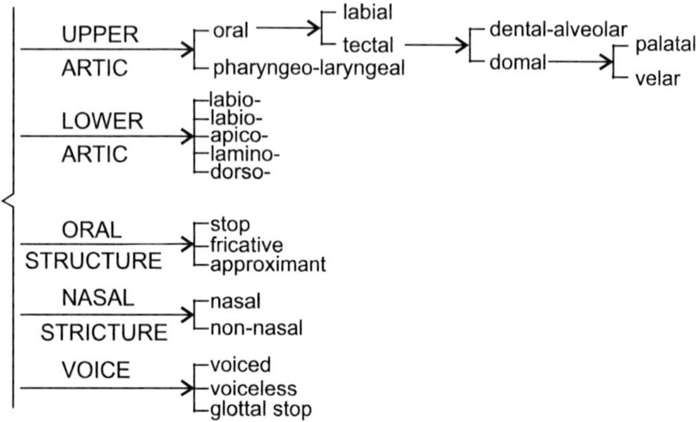

Fig. 6: Phonetic resources

Source: Matthiessen, 1987: 33.

The places of articulation for English nasals /m/, /n/ and /ŋ/ spoken by Indonesian speakers are tabulated in figure 7.[5]

	labial	tectal				
		dental-veolar		domal		
		dental	alveolar	palatal	velar	
stop nasal						voiceless
	m		n		ŋ	voiced

Fig. 7: Places of Articulation of Nasals

Source: Modified from Matthiessen, 1987:38.

5. In Indonesian, palatal nasal is available. And for some consultants in the experiment, /n/ is somehow dental.

The system network of English nasals /m/, /n/ and /ŋ/ spoken by Indonesian speakers is simply given in figure 8 incorporating the table above by specifying only at the edges, i.e. labial, alveolar, and velar.[6]

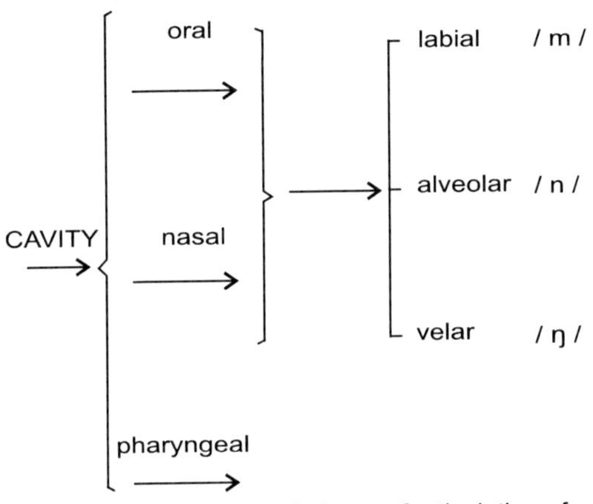

Fig. 8: System Network of places of articulation of nasals

Source: Modified from Matthiessen, 1987.

In the spectrogram observation, it is found that the bar at around 300 Hz supports the idea that voicing basically is not distinctive for English nasals. The system network, then, makes it explicitly by putting pharyngeal unmarked.

The idca of phonetic features emerging a phoneme can be put in a rank as shown in figure 9.

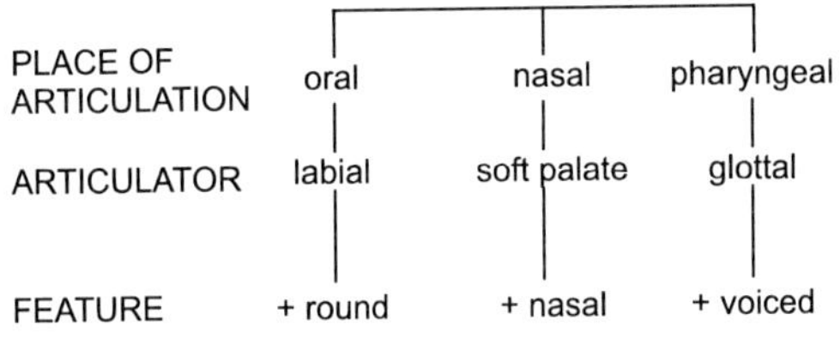

Fig. 9: Phonetic features emerging a phoneme /m/

6. Conclusion

Acoustically, phonetic features can be characterized by the concurrence of particular cues. The investigation of place of articulation as one target in phonetic features within English

6. Pharyngeal is responsible for the terminal feature 'voiced' in the nasal.

nasals spoken by Indonesian is done by observing the spectrograms. Using systemic functional perspective, a system network of places of articulation of the nasals is built up based upon the cues. The system network is, then, meant to fill the gap inter-and-intra stratum in the stratification ranging from phonetics to context. The rank created as the consequence of different constituents (i.e. phonetic features) realizing a wider unit upwards (i.e. phoneme) gives more specification of function in a hierarchy of units. In turn, the value of system network and the notion of rank are considerable in positioning phonetics in the language dimension. The discussion explored above, in fact, does not cover all aspects present in place of articulation within the nasals. However, the selective description hopefully contributes more insights to phonetics and other systemic functional aspects.

References

Abercrombie, David. 1967. *Elements of General Phonetics*. Chicago: Aldine Publishing Company & Edinburgh: Edinburgh University Press.

Catford, J.C. 1977. *Fundamental Problems in Phonetics*. Indiana: Indiana University Press.

——. 1988. *A Practical Introduction to Phonetics*. Oxford: Oxford University Press.

Clark, J. and Collin Yallop. 1990. *An Introduction to Phonetics and Phonology*. Cambridge: Basi Blackwell Inc.

Collin, B. and Inger M. Mees. 2003. *Practical Phonetics and Phonology: A Resource Book for Students*. London: Routledge.

Halliday, M.A.K. & C.M.I.M. Matthiessen, 2004. *An Introduction to Functional Grammar* (3rd edn). London: Arnold.

Halliday, M.A.K. & William S. Greaves. 2008. *Intonation in the Grammar of English*. London: Equinox.

Ladefoged, P. 1996. *Elements of Acoustics Phonetics*. Chicago: The University of Chicago Press.

——. 2000. *Vowels and Consonants*. Oxford: Blackwell Publishing.

Matthiessen, Christian M.I.M. 1987. *Notes on Akan Phonology: A Systemic Interpretation*. MS.

Matthiessen, C.M.I.M. 2007. "The "architecture" of language according to systemic functional theory: Developments since the 1970s". In R. Hasan, C.M.I.M. Matthiessen, J. Webster (eds.) *Continuing Discourse on Language*, Volume 2. London: Equinox: 505-61.

Ohala, J.J. 1997. *Aerodynamics of Phonology*. Proceedings 4th Seoul International Conference on Linguistics.

Stevens, Kenneth N. 1998. *Acoustic Phonetics*. Cambridge, Mass.: MIT Press.

8

Awareness of English Phonetics among English Teachers in High Schools and its Effect on Students' Spoken English

A. Mallikarjunappa

Increasing demand for young graduates with good spoken English skills in the software field and the BPO sector made concerned stakeholders think seriously about the English language and its teaching. A lot of importance was given to spoken skills, intelligibility, mannerisms and also to grammatically correct written English. But, ground situation is different. The majority of professional and general graduates from district headquarters woefully lack these skills. They are good at core subjects but fail in English communication and writing skill. The companies that came down to district headquarters for recruitment were unable to appoint any candidates because of this reason. The present paper is an attempt to study the causes at root level. Indian students do acquire English language skills as second language learners. This acquisition is a process of habit formation and takes its own time. Much of their skills depends on what kind of inputs they obtain during their formative years in their high school studies. To know the quality of teaching—learning process of these skills at the high school level, a survey is undertaken on the awareness of English teachers in schools on different elements of spoken English. For this purpose, a questionnaire was sent to different schools in Bellary, which is a district headquarters in Karnataka with two Engineering colleges, one Medical college and half a dozen Institute of Business studies institutes. The data of this survey throws light on the inputs these students get at high school level. The proposition is that a slight change in awareness, attitude and skills on the part of the teacher would definitely improve the quality of students in spoken English at a young age. This would definitely fetch rich dividends in terms of human resource development in the long run. The survey will point out the areas where the teachers need training and fine tuning within a short time. This will help in designing a short course in Phonetics of English to enable them to give better inputs. The paper also looks into this area of designing a short course as the survey is followed by a two day workshop on phonetics of English for high school teachers of Bellary city.

For this purpose, we have contacted 20 high schools in Bellary city. These include English Medium Convents, English and Kannada Medium aided schools and purely Govt. Kannada Medium Schools. Altogether, 54 teachers responded to the questionnaire. The said questionnaire is aimed at finding the awareness of English teachers in three areas. First seven questions are framed to ascertain their familiarity with vowels, consonants, phonetic symbols and their ability to check the dictionary for correct pronunciation. The next three questions are asked to know the depth of their knowledge in differentiation of voiced and voiceless sounds, transcription, pronunciation of plural and tense markers. Generally, one can attempt these questions if one has undergone a course in phonetics. The third part of the questionnaire is aimed at finding their awareness in the area of accent, rhythm and intonation. All the questions have been framed in multiple choices, objective mode. The outcome is interesting and also encouraging.

Some of the general observations made during the survey are listed as follows:

(a) In almost all schools, there is no concept of English teachers. The English classes are handled by Science,

Mathematics or Social Studies teachers. Some of them felt that English is thrust on them as an additional subject to teach. As much as 75% of responded teachers are not exposed to any kind of course in phonetics in their career.

(b) Many English Medium Convents are recruiting science graduates as English teachers because of their fluency in English. These science graduates are from English medium background and they don't have teaching degree like B.Ed.

(c) English and regional language subjects are considered as of secondary importance both by teachers and students.

(d) The response of young teachers in attempting a number of questions in questionnaire is better when compared to the teachers who have put in long service.

(e) Response to the questionnaire from privately managed English medium convents and aided Kannada and English medium schools is enthusiastic compared to Govt. Schools. Majority of teachers and also Managements have evinced interest to attend the workshop on Phonetics without fail. There is an overall enthusiasm to know the subject as they find it as new area of interest.

(f) Teachers' awareness on accent and consonants is better than vowels, pronunciation and symbols. Very few teachers answered correctly the questions regarding number of vowels in English. This area needs special attention in the workshop.

Some of the conclusions drawn out of the survey are as follows:

(a) 75% of teachers who have answered the questionnaires have not undergone any course in phonetics in their career but around 50% of them said that they are familiar with phonetic symbols and sounds. It seems they have acquired awareness in their teaching career. Many young teachers recruited recently said that they have no familiarity with symbols and sounds. This shows that in course of time, they would pick up these skills.

(b) Almost 50% of respondents answered correctly to the question, how many sounds are there in English language. The other 50% opted for 26 sounds equating sounds with number of alphabet. But, in case of vowels, 83.3%, i.e. 45 out of 54 teachers felt that there are only five vowels in English these include English medium school teachers. But, teachers who have undergone a Phonetics course recently ticked the correct answer, i.e. 20. This shows awareness levels improve dramatically through a short phonetics course.

(c) Interestingly, though 50% of teachers said they have no familiarity with symbols and sounds, all the teachers affirmed that they do consult dictionary for correct pronunciation. Out of 54 respondents, 35 said 'yes' and 19 of them said 'rarely', when asked whether they referred the dictionary for exact pronunciation. It may be because of the fact that some of the dictionaries give pronunciation without the help of symbols and also some give pronunciation in regional languages. At least, majority of them know that the dictionary gives correct pronunciation along with meanings.

(d) There is a strong tendency on the part of teachers to believe that only 'AEIOU' are vowels in English. 98% of teachers opted for the answer of 5 when questioned how many vowels are there in English language.

(e) Only six out of 54 could correctly pick up b*a*t as an answer for the question, could you recognize the vowel used in English but not in Kannada. It shows that 97% of the teachers could not recognize the vowel in b*a*t though they often use it. For the question on diphthong, it was correctly picked up by 20 teachers out of 54. But I have given two correct options. Only five teachers out of 20 ticked both 'boys' and 'made' as the words having diphthong. It shows that many teachers lack awareness in the area of vowels and they pronounce /ei/ as long /e:/ in words like made, cake, so they don't consider /ei/ in made as diphthong. The same tendency is repeated regarding the diphthong /∂ʊ/. Teachers tend to use long /ɔ:/ instead of /∂ʊ/ in words like 'no', 'gold', 'boat', etc. These are some of the areas where a short course on phonetics will be beneficial.

(f) There is a better awareness in usage of consonants by teachers. Surprisingly 37 respondents marked correctly the generally mispronounced consonant by Indian students as /d/ and /Θ/ as in words 'dance' and 'thing'. This shows better awareness of consonants on the part of teachers.

(g) Some questions are asked to test the awareness levels on symbols, transcription, three term labels and differentiating voiceless and voiced sounds. A question on awareness of pronunciation of plurals and past tense markers is set. Almost 50% of the teachers attempted these questions. But it seems many of the teachers haven't got the correct awareness of voiceless and voiced sounds. Majority of teachers have no knowledge of technical terms. Only 9 teachers, i.e. 20% attempted the question on the recognition of fricative sounds. Around 80% did not attempt the question at all. But surprisingly, 42 out of 54 respondents attempted to guess the correct pronunciation of the past tense markers and plurals. But, out of 42 only six teachers got it all correct. This shows that there is enthusiasm to know and guess the correct pronunciation and also there is a faint awareness in this area of pronunciation of past tense and plural markers.

(h) The area which tested on accent and intonation has three questions. Four words are given to mark the stress. Thirty-six respondents attempted this question.

Majority of English medium school teachers showed better awareness compared to others. There is a fair understanding on the part of the teachers in this area. It needs only fine tuning. All the respondents have said that they are aware of intonation.

The overall impression is that teachers of English are enthusiastic to know something in this area. As many as 50 teachers expressed their willingness to participate in a workshop. Some of the Managements of private schools evinced interest to send not only their language teachers but also other subject teachers for the workshop.

We are planning to conduct a two day workshop of six sessions on a weekend, i.e. on Saturday and Sunday.

In the first session, we want to concentrate mainly on familiarizing symbols of vowels. We also want to introduce the position of tongue, mouth and lip in uttering articulation of English vowel sounds.

In the second session, we want to concentrate on symbols of consonants, and also the place and manner of articulation of English consonant sounds. The teacher will come to know the exact manner of pronunciation of sounds and also the difference between voiceless and voiced sounds. This essential information will be an eye opener to them as they can try to form new habit of pronunciation suitable to English sound system. Then they can follow it in their day-to-day classroom teaching. This will help to shape student's pronunciation on the principles of intelligibility to international audience at a very young age. The habit formation would be very easy at an early age.

In the third session, we want to make the whole session an interactive and funny programme. Afternoon session would be a kind of quiz competition among different groups of teachers. They will play games on transcription of words, finding of correct pronunciation of words by consulting dictionary. We thought of giving dictionary to each group. This session will give awareness of phonetic symbols, transcription and also consultation of dictionary for pronunciation. Passages will also be read by teacher. The best reading will be awarded marks and prizes. So a peep will be provided to teachers by the end of the day in the world of phonetics.

The fourth session on the second day morning will be the session on MTI (Mother Tongue Influence). In this session we want to highlight the difference in pronunciation of some sounds in mother tongue, that is, Telugu or Kannada in English. For example, in words like make, cake, the student use long /ɔ:/ instead of diphthong /ei/. The highlighted fact will sink into the minds of experienced teachers so that they can follow it in classroom teaching. Another example would be using long / ɔ:/ in words like no, boat, and gold, instead of /əu/. The same highlighting technique is used regarding consonants. Kannada and Telugu languages use retroflexive /t/ while English language uses alveolar /t/. Likewise, in place of fricative /θ/ the Indian speakers may use plosive /θ/. This can also be made to practise by the teachers then and there itself. These remedial corrections will help a lot in improving the pronunciation aspect of English language by teachers. The awareness of teacher can also be drawn towards correct pronunciation of past-tense marker and plural.

Pronunciation of the Past-tense Marker –d or –ed

The past tense marker –d or –ed is pronounced /-t/, /id/. The choice depends on the sound with which the present tense form ends.

(a) If the present tense ends in voiceless consonants other than /t/ the past tense marker –d or –ed is pronounced /-t/. If the present tense ends in voiced sound other than /d/ the past tense marker is pronounced /-d/. If the present tense ends in /t/ or /d/ the past tense marker is pronounced /-id/.

The fourth session essentially deals with mother tongue influence in spoken English and remedial measures to be taken by English teachers.

The fifth session is a session on stress, accent, rhythm and intonation. We thought of using EFLU (formerly CIEFL) audio cassettes and show them the rhythmic pattern of English language and how they can inculcate that in day-to-day teaching.

The final and sixth session includes practice on all the aspects covered in preceding sessions, group discussions on language issue and opinion collection.

This paper emphasizes the need of short workshops, refresher courses for teachers of English on phonetics to yield qualitative changes in their spoken English that in turn will have effect on young student's skills in English.

QUESTIONNAIRE

Department of English, Veerashaiva College, Bellary

A study of awareness of English phonetics in teachers of English

Dear Teacher friends,

In the background of the global demand for communication skills, we present a questionnaire aimed at making a survey on the degree of awareness of English Phonetics among English teachers. So, kindly co-operate by answering the questions, so as to make proper assessment and find out the remedial need in the area of teaching English language. Please consider it, not as a test of your ability but as a sample survey. We will be grateful and thankful for your co-operation.

Questionnaire

1. Have you undergone any course in English Phonetics in your UG/PG Course, Workshops and Refresher Courses?

   Yes ☐ No ☐

2. Are you familiar with Phonetic symbols of English sounds?

   Yes ☐ No ☐

3. Total number of sounds in English Language including vowels and consonants are:

   25 ☐ 34 ☐ 44 ☐ No Idea ☐

4. How many vowel sounds are there in English?

   5 ☐ 10 ☐ 20 ☐ No Idea ☐

5. Do you refer dictionary to know the exact pronunciation of words?

   Yes ☐ No ☐ Often ☐ Rarely ☐

6. Could you recognize the vowel sound in the words given below which is used in English, but not in Kannada? (Do not answer if you have no idea)

   C<u>o</u>t ☐ B<u>a</u>t ☐ <u>E</u>at ☐ F<u>oo</u>t ☐

7. Could you tick the *words* which contain diphthong? (Do not answer if you have no idea)

   Market ☐ Boys ☐ Mend ☐ Made ☐

8. Can you point out the vowel in the words given below which is normally pronounced wrong by the Indian students? (Do not answer if you have no idea)

   B<u>o</u>at ☐ M<u>ee</u>t ☐ R<u>a</u>t ☐ Th<u>a</u>t ☐

9. Mark the *words* where consonants are generally mispronounced by the Indian students? (Do not answer if you have no idea)

   <u>T</u>ea ☐ <u>D</u>ear ☐ Li<u>p</u> ☐ <u>Th</u>ank ☐

10. Can you mark the symbols given below as voiceless or voiced? (Do not answer if you have no idea)

Example:

	Voiceless	Voiced
/t/	√	
/p/		
/e/		
/v/		
/z/		

11. Please mark some of the fricative sounds. (Do not answer if you have no idea)

   /m/ ☐ /k/ ☐ /f/ ☐ /s/ ☐

12. Which is the correct pronunciation of the following words? (Do not answer if you have no idea)

Example:

Boys				
Capped				
Tables				
Cutlets				

13. Please put the stress mark on the appropriate syllable of the following words (Do not answer if you have no idea)

Example:

Tailor	`tailor
Begin	
About	
Teacher	
Before	

14. Do you read English poems in class with rhyme and rhythm?

Yes ☐ No ☐

15. Are you aware of the falling and rising tone?

Yes ☐ No ☐

16. Do you feel a workshop on English phonetics is necessary?

Yes ☐ No ☐

17. If yes, are you willing to participate?

Yes ☐ No ☐

Thank you for your co-operation. The information collected is purely for academic purposes and it is highly confidential and never shared with anybody.

Name of the Teacher:
Name of the School:
Classes Taught:

Signature

9

Uses of Spoken English in Different Regions of India

Aswini Kumar Mishra

1. Introduction

English has been with India since the early 1600s, when the East India Company started trading and English missionaries first began their efforts. A large number of Christian schools imparting an English education were set up by the early 1800s. The process of producing English-knowing bilinguals in India began with the Minute of 1835, which officially endorsed T.B. Macaulay's goal of forming "a class who may be interpreters between us and the millions whom we govern—a class of persons, Indians in blood and colour, but English in taste, in opinion, in morals and in intellect" (quoted in Kachru 1983, p. 22). English became the official and academic language of India by the early twentieth century. The rising of the nationalist movement in the 1920s brought some anti-English sentiment with it—even though the movement itself used English as its medium.

Once independence was gained and the English were gone, the perception of English as having an alien power base changed; however, the controversy about English has continued to this day. Kachru notes that "English now has national and international functions that are both distinct and complementary. English has thus acquired a new power base and a new elitism" (Kachru 1986: 12). Only about three per cent of India's population speak English, but they are the individuals who lead India's economic, industrial, professional, political, and social life. Even though English is primarily a second language for these persons, it is the medium in which a great number of interactions in the above domains are carried out. Having such important information moving in English conduits is often not appreciated by Indians who do not speak it, but they are relatively powerless to change that. Its inertia is such that it cannot be easily given up. This is particularly true in South India, where English serves as a universal language in the way that Hindi does in the North. Despite being a three per cent minority, the English speaking population in India is quite large. With India's massive population, that three per cent puts India among the top four countries in the world with the highest number of English speakers. English confers many advantages to the influential people who speak it—which has allowed it to retain its prominence despite the strong opposition to English which rises periodically.

2. Purpose and Collection Methods

The English which is spoken in India is different from that spoken in other regions of the world, and it is regarded as the unique variety which is called Indian English. The purpose of this folklore project is to show some of the various ways Indians have intentionally and unintentionally customized English to better suit their needs and to discuss some of the problems and situations which can and do arise when Indians use or experience English in different settings. Attitudes about English and English speakers in India are also explored.

The collecting was done in two separate discussion groups in which various aspects of Indian English were talked about. The first discussion was with N.G., N.J., and S. Shah in their apartment. I had visited them several times before and engaged in lengthy discussions on various issues, so when I came with my recorder in hand and a topic already in mind, very little was needed to establish a good rapport. The second discussion was held with B.C., A.S., and S. Singh in B.C. and S. Singh's apartment—the same apartment that I had lived in for the previous two years with S. Singh as one of my flatmates. With this established link, I had little trouble getting the conversation moving. Languages are often a subject of casual, though often heated, conversations between Indians, so both groups were very interested in the topic. Also, I found that in both groups, individuals were able to play off each other and, in doing so, delve further into the issues than they would have alone. I learned a great deal from the discussions, but I was very thankful for my two years of living with Indians and my month-long trip to India which prepared me for understanding and participating in the discussions. I also received input from several other Indian friends (Murali Kota and Aditya Mulukutla especially) in informal conversations about Indian English.

3. Distinguishing Characteristics of Indian English

Indian English is a distinct variety of the English language. Many Indians claim that it is very similar to British English, but this opinion is based on a surface level examination of lexical similarities. Of course, one must keep in mind that not every linguistic item is used by every Indian English speaker and that a great deal of regional and educational differentiation exists. Even so, items can be identified which are indicative of Indian English speech and which are widely used. These operate on various phonological, morphological, lexical, and syntactic levels, which I will characterize with items brought up in the recorded discussions, in my previous experience with Indian English, and in scholarly writings about Indian English. References to the transcription excerpts (pages 17-26 of this report) are written, for example, as 1.3.4, which indicates Discussion 1, Excerpt 3, Item 4.

4. Phonology

I was able to do very little on the phonological level. I set up a test to see if the English alveolar /t/ would be articulated as the Indian retroflex /t/ or as the dental /t/ in different phonological environments. The result was that the retroflex completely replaced the alveolar; in fact, it has been found that the entire series of English alveolar consonants tends to be replaced by retroflex consonants (Trudgill & Hannah 1994, p. 128). One item that did come out of the experiment was that some Indian English speakers had a tendency to drop the -ed ending after /k/ and /t/ (e.g. walked became walk) (1.6.5). Some interesting things seemed to be happening with the articulation of /ð/ (as in *then*), which normally is pronounced as an inter-dental /d/, but which sometimes seemed to become alveolar. Also, listening to the taped discussions revealed that sometimes *a* was used in front of vowel—initial words (1.4.2) before which North American English and British English speakers would use *an*. This is a very natural adjustment for native speakers, yet it is apparent that a conscious effort to do this is sometimes required by Indian English speakers (2.2.3). To discover whether or not these observations are significant would require further testing.

Other items listed by Trudgill and Hannah (1994) are that Indian English tends to have a reduced vowel system; /r/ tends to become a flap or retroflex flap; the consonants /p/, /t/, and /k/ tend to be un-aspirated; and in some regions, /v/ and /w/ are not distinguished (volleyball is the same as wallyball), while in others, /p/ and /f/, /t/ and /θ/, /d/ and /ð/, and /s/ and /ʃ/ are not (1.4.4). They also note that "Indian English tends to be syllable rather than stress-timed. Also, syllables that would be unstressed in other varieties of English receive some stress in Indian English and thus do not have reduced vowels. Suffixes tend to be stressed, and function words which are weak in other varieties of English (of, to, etc.) tend not to be reduced in Indian English" (p. 128).

5. Morphology

Indian English morphology is very creative and it is filled with new terms and usages. Indian English uses compound formation extensively, as in English-speaking classes (1.3.1) or convent-going (1.2.1). The compounds cousin-brother and cousin-sister allow the Indian English speaker to designate whether their cousin is male or female—a function which is inherent in the terminology of most Indian languages. Others include chalk-piece, key-bunch, meeting notice, age barred, and pindrop silence. Indians also pluralize many English mass nouns and end up with words such as litters, furnitures, and woods (Trudgill & Hannah, pp. 129-30). Sometimes words which should be pluralized are not; for example, S. Shah says, "One of my relative" (1.6.1). A quintessential Indian English term which comes from compound formation is time-pass, which denotes something as non-exciting, as in "That movie was real time-pass." It can also indicate the act of passing time without a specific purpose or motivation.

Indians also shorten many words to create commonly used terms. Enthusiasm is called enthu; as such, it can be used in new ways. One can say, "That guy has a lot of enthu." While this is simply an abbreviation, enthu can also be used as an adjective where enthusiasm cannot, as in "He's a real enthu guy." The same applies for fundamentals, which is shortened as fundas. "She knows her fundas." What is interesting about fundas is that when the -as ending is dropped and -u is added, it takes on a new meaning and can be used in a new way. Fundu basically means wonderful or brilliant. One can say "He is a fundu person" or even "He is fundu."

When bringing Indian words into English, terms such as roti (bread), which are already plural, will be pluralized for English by the addition of -s (rotis). English suffixes are also appended to Indian terms. An example which was brought up in the first discussion is the practice in Bombay of adding -fy to a Hindi word to indicate that an action is being done to someone by someone. From the Hindi word muska, to muskafy means to flatter somebody or to butter them up. Similarly, to pataofy is the action of wooing someone. Other suffixes such as -ic (Upanishadic), -dom (cooliedom), and -ism (goondaism) are used to create new usages for Indian terms. Prefixes can also be used in new ways. In Indian English, pre- is substituted for post- in postpone to create prepone, which indicates, for example, that a meeting has been moved to a sooner time.

6. Lexicon

The Indian English lexicon has many distinct terms which are commonly used by its speakers. Some arise through the use of old and new morphological features, as discussed above. Others come from acronyms and abbreviations. Many terms from Indian languages are utilized, and new usages for English words or expressions are created. It must be noted that many of these terms and usages are specific to the population of Indian English speakers who are currently between twenty and thirty years of age.

Examples of the use of acronyms include the following:

MCP = Male Chauvinist Pig

FOC = Free Of Charge

MPK = Maine Pyar Kiya (a popular movie)

QSQT = Qayamat Se Qayamat Tak (a popular movie)

ILU = I Love You (from a song; pronounced ee-lu)

ABCD = American Born Confused Deshi (native of India)

FOB = Fresh Off the Boat

FOB is actually used by American-born Indians against Indian-born Indians who come to America and tease them for being ABCDs. Other acronyms stem from entire Hindi sentences. Many abbreviations are used by Indians. For example:

Jan = January

Feb = February

subsi = subsidiary

supli = supplementary

soopi = superintendent

princi = principle

Gen. Sec. or G. Sec. = General Secretary

Soc. Sec. = Social Secretary

lab. ass. = laboratory assistant

ass wardi = assistant warden

What is interesting about Indian English abbreviations is that they are pronounced the way they are spelled after they have been shortened. A North American English speaker will generally read an abbreviation as though it were an entire word (i.e. Sec. is read as Secretary). Also, North American English speakers tend to abbreviate phonetically when spoken abbreviations are used (i.e. Soc. is pronounced soash). When read by an Indian English speaker, Soc. Sec. is pronounced sock seck. Actually, many English words which are pronounced quite differently than their spelling would indicate as they are spelled by many Indians. Vowels which have been dropped by North American and British English speakers are typically articulated by Indians. For example, typically is generally pronounced ti-pick-lee, but Indian English speakers will often say ti-pick-ah-lee.

New words and new usages of standard words are introduced as well. A food grinder is simply called a mixi. Jangos are people who are very maud (modern) and fashionable—such people could be described as fast (untraditional and modern). A deadly movie or event is hard-hitting and action-packed. Something which is hi-tech is exceedingly incredible. It is not just limited to technology; for example, one could be wearing a hi-tech outfit. A reception is sometimes called at home. An illiterate person may be called a thumbs-up because they use their thumbprint to sign documents. For an Indian doing math, two into four means "2 x 4" and six by three or six upon three means "6/3". A square root is known as an under root. Sometimes, a series of words is used to approximate a word which momentarily escapes one's mind, such as B.C.s use of "over his self" to mean conceited (2.2.2). Indian English speakers use less to indicate that something is insufficient—"There is less salt in the curry." Often this is extended to too less of. The extraneous of also appears in the expressions too much of and so much of, such as S. Singh's "so much of heat" (2.2.5). None of my informants were sure why of is used in those situations, but they all agreed it did not come from Hindi or any other Indian language's usage.

7. Hindi-Influenced Terms and Expressions in Indian English

Some items are directly related to characteristics of Indian languages. Indians will often ask, "What is your good name?" which is a somewhat literal translation of "Aapka shubh naam kya hai?" Shubh means auspicious or good, and it is basically used as a polite way of asking for someone's full name. An Indian English speaker says today morning (aaj subha) or yesterday night (kal raat) to mean last night. Indians also run the risk of offending Americans when they use certain literal translations which have the intended meaning, but which also have offensive connotations. N.G. mentioned that a U.S. American with whom she works told her that she was an "abrasive woman" because she told him to shut up. Shut up in Hindi is chup bet, which is generally used more casually (but which can be used offensively as well). Also, Indians commonly use "you people" when they want to address more than one person. They do not realize the belittling, racial connotations that it carries with it—for them it is a simple translation of "aap log or tum log". Hindi terms and expressions used in Indian English.

When Indians use English, it is often a mixture of English, Hindi, and other languages. B.C., A.S., and S. Singh called this way of speaking *khichri* (2.2.3). *Khichri* is a meal which is composed of several random ingredients—a rather accurate description of the way Indians often talk to one another. Even in "pure" Indian English, many Indian terms slip in frequently. Some expressions such as general mai (in general) and ek minute (one minute) are prevalent in Indian English. N.G. mentions the Gujarati expression take care karje (do take care) in 1.1.5. These mixtures come quite naturally when one is acquainted with two or more languages. When I began learning Hindi, I acquired many new terms, one of which was mausum (which means weather or season). I unwittingly coined the expression awesome mausum one afternoon when I stepped outside and discovered what a beautiful day it was. N.G. passed this expression along to her friends in Bombay, and supposedly it is starting to spread there. Her use of nahi (no) in 1.1.2, and S. Singh's use of kya (what) in 2.1.1 are typical of the sorts of ways Hindi terms are employed. Other commonly used Hindi terms and expressions include the following:

achchaa = good

arrai = hey

bahut = a lot

bus = that's it

ek = one (as a number)

ghotu = one who reads a lot

hajar (hazar) = a ton (more than a lot)

ho gaya = done; finished

koi bat nahi = no problem

kya hall hai = how are you

lakh(s) = one-hundred thousand

lekin = but

masala = risqué; spicy; hot (like a film)

mutlab = meaning

pakka = pure

teek hai = okay (lit: it is right)

yaar = buddy; pal

These are just a few of the most common ones. One must be fairly conversant with these and other terms and expressions if one wants to follow a discussion between Indians completely.

8. Syntax

Hindi syntax affects Indian English syntax in several ways. There is a seemingly arbitrary use of the articles a and the, which do not have parallels in Hindi. Often, one is substituted for a; for example, S. Shah says "And one black lady..." (1.6.4). The articles "The" and "a" are often dropped when they should be said (1.2.2; 1.6.2; 2.1.2; 2.2.6) and used when they should be left out (1.1.3; 1.4.5; 1.6.3; 2.3.1). It is not uncommon to hear something like, "We are going to temple." Whether or not these apparent misuses are actually arbitrary would require further study. I suspect they are not. Something which Indian English has that is not found in other varieties of English is the use of only and itself to emphasize time and place. It comes from the Hindi words and produces sentences like "I was in Toledo only" and "Can we meet tomorrow itself?" Indian English speakers often use reduplication as a way of emphasizing an action—I have been told before to "Come come! Sit sit!" Reduplication can also replace very for intensifying or extending something, as in hot, hot water and long, long hair. Such usage is common in spoken Hindi. Another thing Indian English speakers do is to leave out when giving a range of numbers. B.C. does this in 2.3.3 when he says, "...two three languages...." This often expresses exaggeration when larger numbers are used, as in "one hundred two hundred."

Certain verbs are used in Indian English in the same way they are used in Hindi. Indians use *kholna* and band *karna* when asking someone to turn a light on or off; the literal translation is retained, so some Indian English speakers say "open the light" and "close the light." The same is true of giving a test (from the Hindi verb *dena*) rather than taking a test. Take means consume when used with food and drink items—"Will you take tea?" The verb *lena* is the Hindi equivalent of this. A.S. elicits another Hindi-based syntactic element, the tag question, in 2.2.4. He says, "Yeah, like this guy Gotham felt like when he went back, no?" This use of no (and the expression isn't it in the same manner) stems from the use of *na* in Hindi, which is exemplified by N.G. in 1.1.6, "...take care *karje applai ker hai na*?" This could be roughly translated as "...take care karje can be applied, can't it?"

Indian English speakers often use certain verbs in ways that are confusing to speakers of other English varieties. Keep is used for put, so one finds Indians saying things like "keep the ball there" or "keep the ball back" to a person who is still holding the ball. Leave replaces keep's lost function of allowing something to remain somewhere. Put is often used without an explicit destination or direction, so an Indian might say, "Shall I put the tape?" or, like B.C. in 2.2.3, "put an image."

One of the most indicative signs of Indian English grammar is the use of the progressive aspect with habitual actions, completed actions, and stative verbs. This produces sentences such as "I am doing it often" rather than "I do it often"; "Where are you coming from?" instead of "Where have you come from?"; and "She was having many sarees" rather than "She had many sarees" (Trudgill & Hannah, p. 132).

The word order of questions is often unique in Indian English. Sentences such as "What you would like to eat?" and "Who you will come with?" show the absence of subject-verb inversion in direct questions. S. Shah provides an example in 1.1.1, "...what is your companion," in which an inversion does not take place where it should. Another aspect of grammar that is often inconsistent is the use of also (a very popular word in Indian English). It can be found in various parts of a sentence, but it tends to be placed at the end, like N.J. does in 1.1.4—"We never even used Hindi word also."

9. Having Fun with English

Indian English speakers play around with the language as much as any other group. English is an important part of life for them, especially in school and when they come to the United States. They circulate documents on their e-mail on things such as a list of ways to change from an Indian conversation to a more American conversation. A common saying among Indian graduate students in the United States jokes about how routine their lives sometimes become:

Apartment, Department. Advisor, Budweiser.

This is joined by other items such as ABCD (mentioned earlier). Actually, ABCD extends to Z, and it makes fun of the Gujaratis who operate motels in the United States:

> American Born Confused Deshi, Emigrated From Gujarat, Housed In Jersey, Kept Lotsa Motels, Named Omkaranath Patel, Quietly Reached Success Through Underhanded, Vicious Ways, Xenophobic Yet Zestful.

Another item utilizes the English alphabet in rhyme: A-B-C-D-E-F-G.

Sheesha mati daru pi. (Drink liquor from a bottle.)

Indians are also acutely aware of the vast differences in accents in spoken Indian English which are caused by India's different linguistic regions. N.G.'s Guju jokes (1.4) are good examples of how Indians make sometimes fun of their own and each other's accents:

> What does a Guju have for breakfast? Snakes. (Snacks) (1.4.1). What does an eighties Guju wear? Foos nu pant and smace nu shirt. (F'us pants and a Smash shirt) (1.4.3). What does a nineties Guju wear? Jins jicket, low loacket. Comb in bayck poaket, and goagles on eye soaket. (Jeans jacket, love locket, comb in back pocket, and goggles on eye socket) (1.4.6).

10. Encountering North American English and the United States

Indians are very cognizant of the differences between North American English and Indian English. Those who come here find themselves bombarded by new expressions, new terms, and new slang. Often these are simply lexical differences between North American English and British English (with which Indian English has more terms in common), but sometimes Indians can be surprised when they try to translate a North American English expression into their own languages. S. Shah related a story to one of her relatives who ran into this problem:

> One of my relatives was here before a few years ago, and he was kind of new. I mean, he just came to U.S., and he didn't know how to speak English, and he was just kind of new. So, he was going to somewhere in Chicago. He was traveling by the train, and he was sitting on the seat somewhere over there. And one black lady came up to him and asked him, "What's up?" And in Gujarati what's up means like *upar shuche* (Gujarati: what is above you). So he made it into Gujarati, so he said, "The sky." So that lady gave him ten cents and went away (1.6).

Some Indians whose names have similar sounding words in English find U.S. Americans poking fun at them. One example is A.S.'s uncle Shambu, who was called Shampoo when he came to the United States (2.2.1). A friend of mine whose name is Mani was constantly chided by U.S. Americans because "it's always great to have Money around!"

There are also many regional stories and jokes about certain individuals who have gone to the United States and come back talking and acting in a peculiar manner. N.G. recounted the story of a fellow who seemed to think of himself as other than Indian when he returned from the United States, which he showed by speaking in English and using the possessive "your" when refering to India: "There was this guy who stayed for some years in America though it was very difficult to go there (the USA) at that time. So, when he came back, he was wearing this really thick, woollen jacket around, and sporting it around though it was summer. He was walking around with it, and he kept saying, "Your India is so hot! Your India is so hot!" So it's like, yeah, every time it's really hot in the house and people are complaining about it, that's what we say. "Oh, your India is so hot!" Ay, he was wearing a jacket, I mean he had no reason to complain" (1.5).

11. Using English in India

As noted earlier, English is not appreciated by many Indians who consider it an elite, oppressive language. It is used by many upper class Indians to show off their status. All of my informants agreed that while many people respect a person for being able to speak English, they also feel that English-speakers are snobbish (1.2; 2.3). In fact, using English in the wrong situations can lead to a serious scolding, as B.C. discovered in Tirupathi:

> Like it happened once with me. I am not very familiar with my mother tongue. So I'd been to this holy place of Tirupathi. Okay? So I went there, and this was the time I went alone. And I didn't know how to converse with him properly. Basically, the thing out there is between Tamil and Telugu, it's a bit mixed, ah, up, you know, the dialect. So I was trying to converse with him and I wasn't successful, so I thought I'd do it in English. So I started talking to him in English, and like that fellow got really pissed. He was telling—like he was real mad. If you don't know, just get out, or something like that. It was all for booking of a silly room. That's it. All I had to do was get a room (2.1).

Such reactions mostly depend on the individual attitude of the person one is dealing with. However, it seems that a person is given respect not only for knowing English, but also for knowing when to use it.

12. Speaking English Correctly

My background experience with Indian English allowed me to notice that in the taped discussions, certain attempts were made by individuals to speak more "properly" and with fewer Indian terms and slang words. Indian English as it is spoken between Indians is quite different from what I recorded during the discussions. One obvious reason for this was my presence as an active participant in the discussion, thereby necessitating the use of English in a way that would be understandable to me. Another reason is that there is a predominating preoccupation with many Indians in regard to approximating British English when they are speaking—particularly when they are conversing with a native North American English or British English speaker. Outright discussions about the correctness of a particular word or usage arose several times during both discussions (1.3.2).

I am often told quite earnestly by many Indians that their English is more like British English than North American English is. They cite many examples of words they use in common with the British—not realizing that when analyzed on deeper linguistic levels, Indian English differs from British English just as much as North American English. The question to raise then is—who really cares what is correct? They are all mutually distinct varieties, and that uniqueness should be valued and appreciated. Even so, many Indians seem to hold British English up as the paragon; perhaps this is because how well one approximates British English often determines how well one's educational level is regarded in India.

13. Conclusion

This leads to the question—do Indians appreciate their own English? Ultimately, I think they do. It has been said that Indians have made English into a native language with its own linguistic and cultural ecologies and socio-cultural contexts. My informants indicated that in many ways, Indian English is very much their own. Its special functions have engraved English into the cultural life of India, and it is very much a part of the experience of being Indian—even if one does not speak it. Many Indians feel that the use of English should actively be encouraged because of the many advantages it confers—the greatest of which is its universal character. The Indian writer and philosopher Raja Rao wrote:

> Truth, said a great Indian sage, is not the monopoly of the Sanskrit language. Truth can use any language, and the more universal, the better it is. If metaphysics is India's primary contribution to world civilization, as we believe it is, then must she use the most universal language for her to be universal.... And as long as the English language is universal, it will always remain Indian.... It would then be correct to say as long as we are Indian—that is, not nationalists, but truly Indians of the Indian psyche—we shall have the English language with us and amongst us, and not as a guest or friend, but as one of our own, of our caste, our creed, our sect and our tradition (quoted in Kachru 1986, p. 12).

Many others fear, perhaps legitimately, the loss of India's native languages. English has changed Indian languages in many ways—mostly through the incorporation of new words. However, the population of English speakers in India, though socially influential, is a small minority compared to the rest. Also, most of these individuals are conversant with at least one, if not two or three, other languages, and unless the situation necessitates English, they usually speak in their native language. Even N.G., who approximates British English very closely, would switch to Gujarati when asking for confirmation from N.J. or S. Shah (1.1.6). It seems that multiple languages can function together when they have their particular domains of use. The sheer number of speakers of India's native languages more or less ensures that they do not face extinction.

English is in a slightly more precarious position. Although it has a strong base in the elite class of India and in the general culture, it could easily fall victim to an anti-English movement —if one ever arose. Public fervor is known to be especially forceful in India, and a skillful leader could use it to create such a movement. Hopefully, this will not happen. Indians have a lot to gain from knowing English, and the world has a lot to gain from Indians' knowing English. Some Indians complain that English brings in too much Western thought, but English in India also exports a vast amount of Indian culture and thought to the rest of the world. This increases the diversity of experience that people around the world receive as part of their education. Rather than worrying about whether or not English should be used, people should focus on extending an education to more children which allows them to learn and use English, and which also puts a great emphasis on using and understanding their native languages.

Works Cited

Brunvand, Jan. (1986). *The Study of American Folklore*. New York: W.W. Norton & Company.

Kachru, Braj. (1983). *The Indianization of English*. Oxford: Oxford University Press.

——. (1986). *The Alchemy of English: The Spread, Functions and Models of Non-Native Englishes*. New York: Pergamon Press Inc.

Pandey, D.P. and V.P. Sharma (1993). *English-Hindi Dictionary*. New Delhi: Harper Collins Publishers.

Trudgill, Peter, and Jean Hannah (1994). *International English: A Guide to the Varieties of Standard English*. London: Edward Arnold.

10

Spoken English in Engineering Curriculum: Facts and Fiction

Arabati Pradeep Kumar

Language is the chief medium of communication among human beings. Man has been using language as a tool of communication for centuries. It has enabled him to interact with the environment and to regulate his social behaviour. Man reciprocates his feelings, ideas, thoughts, notions, etc. with others employing language as the most widely used instrument. He communicates meaning through a sophisticated system of symbols. In this research article, we are only concerned with linguistic communication. The word 'communication' is derived from the Latin term *communicare* or *communico*, both of which mean 'to share'. But communication is not only transmission of meaning from one person to another through symbols but also implies that the system of communication is commonly owned, accepted, and recognized by the members of a community. It enables them to acquire, exchange, store, retrieve and process information. Therefore, communication is essentially a social affair. Communication is the modus operandi of social and commercial intercourse.

What is essential for communication to occur is that the cooperation between two parties, one active or at the giving end and the other passive or at the receiving end. The sender selects appropriate symbols to suit the situation and realizes the meaning through speech or writing depending on the socially regulated requirements or self-perceived needs. In the world of today, which is veritably a global village, communication skills are of paramount importance as the means for development and empowerment. The art of communication involves mastery of listening, speaking, reading and writing. Every professional needs to possess competence in communication to make an impressive impact on the global scenario. The English language has been gaining greater importance for the global communication. It is also called the *lingua franca* of the world. It is no longer just a library language or a window to the world but a language of opportunities. A fairly high degree of proficiency in English and excellent communication skills enhance the students' employability. Phonetics develops students' ability to use English accurately, appropriately and fluently both for face-to-face and telephonic communication in academic, social and working situations.

In the curriculum of Engineering colleges affiliated to Jawaharlal Nehru Technological University (JNTU), Andhra Pradesh, the following are included as part of English Language Communication Skills Lab:

1. Introduction to the Speech Sounds (International Phonetic Alphabet Chart)
2. Introduction to Word Stress and Intonation

The English language teacher should familiarize the students with the following facts while teaching English at professional level. But most of the teachers ignore teaching them.

The Use of Basic Knowledge of Phonetics

Phonetics is the study of speech sounds. Phonetics not only describes and discusses the production and a transmission of different speech sounds, but also addresses itself to a host of other aspects of words and sentences and their pronunciation patterns. With a basic knowledge of Phonetics and a bit of conscious practice, one can become a better speaker of English language.

Speech Mechanism

English uses pulmonary-aggressive air-stream mechanism for the production of its speech sounds. This means all English speech is made with the help of the stream of air coming out of the lungs. The human voice works on the same principle as any musical wind instrument. The air coming from the lungs is changed into a sound by an organ called larynx present in the throat. Various organs of speech present in the mouth also participate in the production and transmission of different speech sounds. Also present in the throat, on top of the wind pipe, are a pair of lip-like structure called vocal cords. The vibration of the vocal cords plays an important role in speech. They have two functions:

(i) They determine the pitch of our voice, and

(ii) They give voice to our speech sounds, i.e. they determine whether a speech sound is voiceless or voiced.

General Indian English (GIE)

In India, one may come across many accents of English spoken in different states. Some of these so diverge from one another that they may largely remain mutually unintelligible. Nevertheless, there has evolved, over the years, one variety of English largely acceptable among most of the educated speakers of English who use it. This is General Indian English.

The American Model

In these days of Americanization, the American variety of English is gaining more and more prominence. These days, strong claims are being made in favor of American English as a standard model.

Received Pronunciation (RP)

The choice of many educated speakers of English around the world is RP or Received Pronunciation, the word received here suggesting its social acceptance. This is a better model for Indian speakers for well-known historical reasons.

I. Introduction to Sounds of English

The written forms of most languages of the world are a representation of their spoken forms. Nevertheless, there exists no perfect correspondence between the spelling and the sound in any language. Because of this mismatch between the spelling and the sound, a learner cannot know how to pronounce a new word encountered in his reading; nor can he decide how to spell a new word heard by him. To overcome this problem, phoneticians have evolved an alphabet called the "International Phonetic Alphabet" (IPA). With the symbols and diacritics this alphabet provides, it is possible to transcribe words of any language of the world to write them as they are pronounced. Such a writing is called "Phonetic Transcription." It makes speech visible, thereby making it possible to provide pronunciation of words in dictionaries.

There are forty-four phonetic sounds in the English language and twenty are vowel sounds. Of these twenty, the first twelve are pure vowels or monophthongs and the remaining eight are long vowels or diphthongs. Vowel sounds are free-flowing sounds in the sense air comes out without any friction when these sounds are spoken. There are 24 consonant sounds and these sounds are produced with a friction, i.e. when these sounds are produced any two organs of speech in the mouth come into a contact and produce some friction. Daniel Jones said that "Sounds are heard. Letters are seen. Letters provide a means of symbolizing the sounds. If they do so in a logical manner—in other words, if the essential sounds of any particular language or dialect are represented consistently—the writing is said to be PHONETIC".

Disparities between spelling and pronunciation systems

It is common knowledge that English spelling and pronunciation systems are not consistent with each other, i.e. there is no one-to-one correspondence between the alphabet and the sounds they represent. While English language uses 44 sounds, its alphabet has only 26 letters. In English, very often:

(i) The same letter(s) stand(s) for different sounds.

(a) the letters *ch* stand for different sounds in the words *machine, monarch, chief, chemistry* and *church.*

(b) the letter *a* stands for different sounds in the words *late, last, fat, woman, village, water* and *what.*

(c) the letters *ough* stand for different sounds in the words *though, through, bought, thorough* and *cough.*

(ii) The same sound is represented by different letters or combination of letters.

(a) the /*n*/ sound is represented by n in neck, nn in funny, gn in sign, kn in know and pn in pneumonia.

(b) the vowel sound /*e*/ is represented by the letter e in end, ea in head, ei in leisure, eo in leopard, a in many, ai in said, ie in friend, u in bury and ue in guess.

(c) the vowel sound /i:/ is represented by the letters ea in beat, ie in brief, eo in people, e in scene, ee in seen, ey in key, i in machine, oe in foetus, ei in receive and uay in quay.

(iii) One letter of the alphabet stands for a sequence of two sounds.

(a) the letter q stands for /k/ and /w/ in the words question, quite and square.

(b) the letter x stands for a sequence of /k/ and /s/ in the words excuse, excite and extra.

(c) the letter x stands also for a sequence of /g/ and /z/ in the words exact, examine and exist.

(d) the letter u sometimes stands for a sequence of /j/ and /u:/ in the words unit, use and utilize.

Engineers have to interact with other professionals. They may get a job outside their state, seek an appointment outside India or be sent abroad by the organization where they are working. Under these circumstances, there cannot be proper communication unless their speech is intelligible. To serve this purpose, engineers should aim at good pronunciation. This does not mean that they should speak like Englishmen. The only objective should be to make their speech pleasing and acceptable to people around them.

It is the responsibility of an English teacher to be more practical-oriented while teaching English in engineering colleges. The classroom must be two-way interactive, i.e. learner-centred and teacher-centred. Today, English teachers simply teach all Sounds of English—Vowels, Diphthongs and Consonants with chalk-and-talk-method. Besides teaching them, the teacher should expose the students in the English laboratory where they can learn the transcription of different English words as dictated by the teacher, and also by referring to pronouncing dictionary software. Even the teacher should select most difficult words to be pronounced and pronounce them in the classroom. This will enable the students to understand the pronunciation of difficult words. The English teacher is not trying to make the students understand the aforementioned disparities in pronunciation to dispel the confusion in learning them with more practical bent of mind. The teacher is failing to provide considerable practice to the students during lab periods.

II. Introduction to Word Stress

There are two different kinds of stresses in English, word stress and sentence stress. Both are essential to communicate meaning satisfactorily and both cause many foreign learners of English considerable problems.

Concept of word-stress—Its importance

The syllables of a word can be spoken with more or less force or emphasis. Where a syllable is spoken with emphasis, it is said to be stressed. Syllables that are not spoken with emphasis are unstressed. Not all syllables in an utterance are spoken with equal emphasis. There are certain syllables that are stressed more than others. Thus in the word 'father', the first syllable 'fa-' is stressed and so is spoken more prominently than the second syllable '-ther'. Similarly, in the word 'about', the second syllable is stressed and so is spoken more prominently than the first syllable. We shall now look at some common words to note the syllabic stress patterns. The accent mark is put before the syllable stressed.

Stress patterns

Stress in English words varies from word to word. In some words, the stress falls on the first syllable while in other, it may fall on the second, third, or the fourth syllable.

Sentence stress

Connected speech in English has its own patterns of accent. Words that are important for meaning—content words like nouns, adjectives, principal verbs and adverbs—are generally accented. Grammatical words like articles, personal and relative pronouns, auxiliary verbs, prepositions and conjunctions are generally not accented.

The situation is complicated by the fact that sentences, too, are stressed to underline their meaning. Sentence stress is very important since we use it to communicate part of the meaning of the sentence. It also determines the rhythm of our speech. Normally, certain words in a sentence are spoken more loudly than the others. In the sentence "We are going to Spain for a holiday" the word Spain takes the primary stress, if the sentence is spoken in normal circumstances. However, when the speaker wishes to emphasize the fact that they are travelling to Spain for a holiday and not on business, the sentence may be spoken like this, stressing the last part of the sentence "We are going to Spain on a holiday".

To learn the word accent the teacher should select a few words having two syllables and polysyllabic words and should read out in the classroom. The students should repeat each word after the teacher, either in unison or individually, taking turns. What the teacher generally does is that he goes to classroom and teaches only the rules of word stress and completes it without practice by students. The teacher should say each word twice and the student must say whether the accent is on the first or second syllable. The test of aural training is lacking in the classroom of an engineering college.

The teachers are not putting the students to a test of the production of correct accentual patterns. Students must be asked to read aloud these words with the correct accentuation.

In teaching sentence stress, the teacher should read each sentence and the students should be asked to repeat, taking special care (i) to put the accent on the correct syllable of the word, and (ii) to make the tonic syllable clearly more prominent than all the other syllables in the sentence. The practice as mentioned above is absent in today's teacher's teaching sentence-stress in the classroom.

III. Introduction to Intonation

To enable the learners familiarize themselves with the use of the tunes/tones. We have already seen the vibrating glottis which provides, in sounds, the voiced-voiceless distinction. However, it has another important role to play in continuous speech, i.e., it provides pitch fluctuation. By pitch fluctuation, we mean that the pitch of the voice is continually in the process of either falling or rising while we are talking. In fact, it never remains constant for more than a fraction of a second. Pitch fluctuation is found in the speech of all communities. It is not a random fluctuation but follows well-defined melodic patterns, which are meaningful.

Pitch of the voice

The pitch of the voice is determined by the frequency of the vibration of the vocal cords, i.e. the number of times they open and close in a second. The patterns of variation of the pitch of the voice (i.e. the fall or the rise) constitute the *intonation* of a language. If you say, put it *down!* the pitch of your voice will move from a high level to a low level. This is called the "falling tone". It can be illustrated thus:

E.g.: Put it

d

o

w

n!

If you say the same sentence with a rising tone, the pitch of your voice will move from low to high, as shown below:

E.g.:

n!

w

o

d

Put it

Tune/tone shapes

The number of important words in a word group decides the shape of a tune (tone) and by the attitude you wish to express. By important words, we mean the words which carry most of the meaning in a group. For example, in answer to the question "How was Sheila?" you say, "She was in an appallingly bad temper"—the first four words are not especially helpful to the meaning, i.e. they are not important. But the last three words are important: each of them adds to the picture you are giving of Sheila. Let us see how it might be said:

E.g.: She was in an appallingly **bad**

t

e

m

p

e

r.

So the most important word in this group is *temper* and this decides the shape of the tune.

Before we talk about the speakers' attitude(s) let's see what tunes you must learn to use while speaking English. We cannot teach you all the tunes that English speakers use, but we will describe the ones that we feel you must know.

The falling tune

The *falling tune* is sometimes referred to as the *glide-down*. It consists of a fall in the pitch of the voice from a high level to a low level. It is marked [\ ].

The falling tune is normally used in:

1. Ordinary statements made without any implications, e.g.:
   a. I 'liked it very \much.
   b. It was 'quite \good.
2. Questions beginning with a question-word such as *what, how, where, why,* etc. when said in a neutral way, e.g.:
   a. 'Who were you \ talking to?
   b. 'What's the \ matter?
3. Commands, e.g.:
   a. 'Go and 'open the \window.
   b. 'Take it a\way.
4. Exclamations, e.g.:
   a. \Splendid!
   b. \How extraordinary!
5. Question tags: when the speaker expects the listener to agree with him, e.g.:
   a. It's pleasant to'day, \isn't it?
   b. It was a 'good film, \wasn't it?
6. Rhetorical questions, e.g., where the answer is obvious:
   a. Isn't that \kind of her?
   b. Wasn't that a \difficult exam?

(Note: ['] before a syllable indicates that the following syllable is stressed.)

The rising tune

The *rising tune* is sometimes referred to as the *glide-up*. It consists of a rise in the pitch of the voice from a low level to a high level. It is marked [ˏ]

The rising tune is normally used in:

1. Incomplete statements, e.g.:
   a. It's 'seven 'o ˏclock (and she hasn't got up as yet).
   b. I'll 'buy you a ˏdress (if I go there).
2. Polarity type questions which demand a yes/no answer, e.g.:
   a. 'Are they /coming?
   b. 'Will you ˏdo it?
3. Non-polarity (wh-type) questions when said in a warm/friendly way, e.g.:
   a. 'How's your ˏ daughter?
   b. 'What's the ˏ matter?
4. Polite requests, e.g.:
   a. 'Go and 'open the ˏwindow.
   b. 'Take it a ˏway.
5. Question tags: when the speaker gives his/her listener the option to disagree with him/her,
   a. You're a ˎgardener, ˏaren't you?
   b. It was a ˎgood ˎfilm, ˏwasn't it?
6. Repetition questions, e.g.:
   (John told me to do it.) Who told ˏyou?
7. Expected responses, e.g.:
   ˏThank you.

(If you wish to express real gratitude, you should say *thank you* with a falling tune. A rising tune shows a rather casual acknowledgement of something not very important.)

8. Alternative questions, e.g.:
   a. Do you like ˏtea, ˏcoffee or ˎcoke?
   b. 'Shall we ˏdrive or go by ˎtrain?
9. Enumeration, e.g.:
   One ˏtwo, ˏthree, ˏfour, ˎfive.

10. Afterthought, doubt, hesitation, e.g.:
    a. I'd 'buy a \new one, if I could af /ford it.
    b. In 'spring it 'rains a \lot, /generally.
11. Greetings, partings, apologies, encouragement, e.g.:
    a. Hel/lo.
    b. Good /bye.
    c. I'm so /sorry,
    d. You ought to keep on /trying.

The falling-rising tune [V]:

The last of the tunes that you must learn is the *falling-rising* tune. This tune is sometimes referred to as the *dive*. It consists of a fall from high to low and then a rise to the middle of the voice. This tune can be used on either one syllable or different syllables of a word or sentence. It can be illustrated thus: A few examples pertaining to the falling-rising tune are mentioned below. They are:

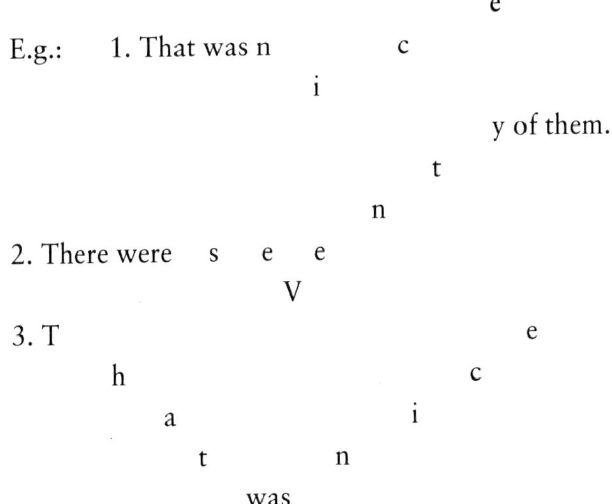

If the fall is on one syllable and the rise begins on a later syllable it is referred to as a divided fall-rise. Sentence 3 is an example of this.

If the fall-rise is used on two different words in a sentence it is marked as in the following example:

\That was, nice.

The falling-rising tune is normally used for special implications not verbally expressed. For example if you say

She's \beautiful.

With a falling tune you mean precisely that. But if you say the same sentence with a falling-rising tune

She's beautiful.

You imply something—perhaps that she is beautiful, but not intelligent. Consider the following examples in which the falling-rising tune is used to convey special implications, e.g.:

a. I am waiting (so do hurry up).
b. I haven't much appetite (but I'll join you to be polite).
c. The *houses* are nice (but perhaps people are not).

This tune can also be used for correcting what someone has said and as a warning, e.g.:

a. (He's forty-five.) Forty-six.
b. (I like him a lot.) You used to like him.
c. *Please* be careful.

As a part of practice, the students must repeat the sentences, given by the teacher, having the individual words and the tone groups in which they occur as nucleus. The students must be sure to use the tone, either falling or rising, as indicated, and be sure to put the nucleus on the correct syllable in each longer utterance. The teacher must read each sentence twice from the marked texts. Students must be asked to underline the tonic syllable (the nucleus) in each sentence as given by the teacher. Students must be asked to read these sentences with the correct accentuation as marked, taking particular care to put the nucleus on the syllable marked. But the English teacher teaching in engineering colleges merely goes to the classroom, and theoretically teaches what intonation is and how it is used in different contexts. If theoretical teaching is not followed by pragmatic approach with suitable pedagogical methodology, the students cannot be benefited in learning word stress and intonation very effectively. This practical approach by constructively using the aids of the language lab is lacking in almost all the engineering colleges. The Ear Training to learn aural skills is quite indispensable without which teaching or learning the word stress and intonation will be incomplete.

Most of the problems pertaining to grammar can usually be sorted out with explanations, a good grammar book and enough practice. Controlled reading and writing help students understand and use grammar better. Guided speaking activities can help improve their spoken language. Pronunciation problems can usually be sorted out through constant and continual drills. However, some of the pronunciation errors are very deeply ingrained and at times it may take specialized accent neutralization classes to get rid of strong accents. The man who can think and does not know how to express what he thinks is at the same level who as the person cannot think.

Conclusion

My paper highlights the facts and fiction of English curriculum in engineering colleges. The core aspects of concentration on listening and speaking as learning skills are dealt with in the paper. Speaking and listening carry a lot of weightage in the chances of employment in the global village. Speaking as an active skill depends largely on listening as passive skill. All aspects covering stress, intonation and pace of delivery and awareness to different accents and problems faced in these areas are highlighted in the paper. How English curriculum in Engineering colleges is different from fact to fiction is taken up in practical classroom situations.

Works Cited

Balasubramanian, T. *A Text Book of English Phonetics for Indian Students*. Madras: MacMillan, 1981.

Farhathullah, T.M. *Communication Skills for Technical Students*. Chennai: Orient Longman, 2002.

Hosali, Priya, and S.V. Parasher. *General Introduction: Phonetics and Spoken English (Block I)*. Hyderabad: CIEFL, 1995.

Madhukar, R.K. *Business Communication*. New Delhi: Vikas Publishing House, 2006.

Mohan, Krishna, and Meera Banerjee. *Developing Communication Skills*. Delhi: MacMillan, 2001.

Rizvi, M. Ashraf. *Effective Technical Communication*. New Delhi: Tata McGraw-Hill, 2007.

Sehgal, M.K., Vandana Khetarpal. *Business Communication*. New Delhi: Excel Books, 2009.

Sethi, J., P.V. Dhamija. *A Course in Phonetics and Spoken English*. New Delhi: Prentice, 2004.

Subba Rao, A.V. et al. *Language as Communication and Structure of Modern English*. Hyderabad: Osmania University.

Varshney, R.L. *An Introductory Text Book of Linguistics and Phonetics*. Bareilly: Student Store, 1993.

11

Challenges Faced by the Indian Professionals in Pronouncing the English Sounds in the BPOs and Corporates

Mousumi Dash and *Monalisa Mishra*

The phenomenal use of English language in the BPO's and Corporate organizations is determined by the English proficiency that directly affects the wage gains and other desirable perks and promotions. Leveraging of English as a medium to outsource services has become a religious recruitment across the globe; and has lured millions of young Indian graduates to be a part of an emerging trend of globalization and transactional communication. Today's young generation has realized the potential of English language as the ultimate platform of personal and professional growth.

But years of nativization and fosilization of the L1 (MTI) factor has posed threats to the upcoming corporate generation. The non-native influence is manifold, semantic, phonological, psychological, social, etc. resulting only in a great cross cultural fissure, misunderstandings and miscommunication, the most explicit and stated are the "phonetic differences". This paper aims at bringing out the missing links and formidable gaps that are created during a corporate transaction or an outsourcing effort and shall focus on identifying the problem sounds of vowels, consonants and glides/diphthongs in context to appropriate examples. Being aware of these problems, we will be able to avoid any sort of confusion at workplace thereby understand others and being understood correctly. This will help us to create a common platform on which the Indian speakers, can pronounce the sounds of English where the receiver understands and decodes the ideas exactly as they are being encoded by the sender.

The employee attribution of the Human Resource Departments focuses on the communication, interpersonal skills to thrive in the service sector. In view of this fact the point becomes conspicuous that all leading professional companies want their potential workforce to be efficient and adept in the areas of understanding the dynamics of management that includes customer dealings, objection handling, conflict management, negotiating, decision-making, etc.

But a clinching factor in riding up the corporate ladder is the non-execution or inability of the above stated skills that mostly get mis-communicated because of poor phonetic quotient, not only by the Indians but also around the globe.

We collected the following realia as an authentic instance of the corporate inefficacy.

Kalyan Das working as a corporate agent for ING Vysya insurance group has meetings with seniors and delegates to discuss a new project. He has to perform the crucial role of negotiating and making that corporate presentation...he is high spirited, confident and outgoing personality type and normally casts a good impression. But conversely his manner of articulation leaves the board of directors puzzled and amused. It is worse when delegates happen to come from the overseas.

His senior associates decipher this as a phonetic malfunction and ask him to seek phonetic correction and assistance from the premiere spoken English institutes.

Example No. 2

Seema works as a liaisoning officer in Kotak Money, a trading organization. She handles telephonic calls from the clients in three languages, i.e. Oriya, English and Hindi. Non-

Oriya speakers usually would converse in English and therein starts the problem with Seema. She gets nervous, uncertain of what she would speak, fumbles, stammers and even if she speaks a flaw is too obviously generated. Clients express the need to replace her. She is depressed and has lost her enthusiasm to take further calls. She even wanted a change in the domain of her work-type.

A survey conducted by us in Vodaphone Telecalling center also showed that the CSAT (customer satisfaction) towards attendees of calls in English was typically less than the CSAT score of the Oriya/Hindi call attendees.

Our findings thus have a clear focal point that hints at the inefficacy of speaking English as the official language. Akhilesh discovers to his awe that in spite of being a terrific presenter he seriously lacked a phonetic quotient. The voice/accent trainers examine his fossilized patterns of typical sounds (the mother togue influence—MTI) and incorrect word stress. To his amazement he did not master at sound English. In fact he was amused with the actual sounds (the correct pronunciation he heard).

The gap needed to be minimized and Akhiliesh wants that crucial promotion. Seema too has decided to boost her confidence and personality by taking remedial spoken English classes where telephonic calls in English, phone etiquettes and other communication tools would be tipped to her. She plans to join a bigger company if she could fare well. The H.R. personnel of Vodaphone have been called in for a special training to enhance the proficiency of the attendees of English speaking customers.

As addressed earlier the focus of this paper is to identify the linguistic (phonetic) challenges (to be precise) faced by Indian corporate and officials. As we treated our findings and deduced the causal factors were manifold.

Firstly, the globalized business environment has posed a heterogeneous combination of culture, attitudes, multilingual differences (dialectical/accentual), norms, stereotypism, ethnocent racism to name a few. Mention should also be made of the emotional, psychological, social factors that affect the above. Today's corporate has to be an amalgamate of all the mentioned features to be professional. Professional or Perishable? A smart answer beckons for a repetoire of effective communication/soft skills, an E.Q., a sound phonetic quotient and a positive attitude.

Secondly the awareness of the complexity involved in the foreign language learning lies on the great variety of elements like listening, vocabulary, grammar, reading, writing. A holistic schema of these combinations is remotely accessed.

The feasible solutions that can be worked out would therefore require attention on the following elements. As Myriam Lemay would put it, a non-native speaker should undergo a rigorous articulatory workout—identify the phonetic pitfalls, enhance vocabulary, plan a phonetic correction, control breathing, practise stress and intonation for the coveted results.

The phonetic correction would involve the following:

1. Checking Erroneous Pronunciation

English words are not spelt as they are pronounced in most Indian languages; car-ka: with the aspiration h, Hindi pronunciation would be kaar with close ended consonant/ consonant clusters.

A common practice that lurks with many is writing exactly as the word is spelt and in turn pronouncing it as it is written.

Literal translation of word meanings thereby obstructing the flow of ideas and phonetic pace.

2. Ignorance of Spelling

A poor schema of spelling (often resulting from poor reading) may leave us uncued as to what should be the correct pronunciation. A dictionary can serve a messiah as the phonemic transcription gives the exact sound of the word along with the meaning. This could save the morpheme-grapheme omission/insertion, silencing (laterals). In fact knowledge of morpheme/grapheme may enhance the correct pronunciation.

3. Stress/Intonation

English being a stressed timed language unlike Indian languages being syllable timed language efforts should be taken so as to sound natural by stressing the right sound for a meaningful utterance. Cases of faulty meanings being exchanged may seriously affect transactions. Similarly intonation may make or mar meanings and moods of the speakers.

4. Universal Appeal: Phonic Saavy

Culturing a sensible and sensitive attitude towards the dichotomical differences of vowel and consonants, stressing/intonating enhances the phonetic performance. Corporate houses also allege of attitudinal influences of employees that damage the phonetic representations.

5. Overgeneralization

A fatal tendency of overlooking errors and the set of rules, a casual approach may only lead to more fossilization; let alone improvement.

Having identified the bottlenecks of phonetic correction (the entire capsule discussed above) it becomes essential for the corporate house to identify, address, establish the cause, determine the objective, choose the appropriate technique and finally workout the correction.

12

The Utility Value of Language Laboratories in Teaching Phonetics and Spoken English

R.V. Jayanth Kasyap

The oft used terms in ELT these days are CALL and CALT (Computer-Aided Language Learning and Computer-Aided Language Training). Technology-driven classrooms play a significant role in the acquisition of language skills. Today almost all the conventional and technological universities made the lab component a mandatory item of the English curriculum. Beyond doubt this advancement yielded fruitful results. But it also gave scope for certain unhealthy trends. Serious questions about the overdose and overuse of self instructional and user friendly software continue to draw the attention of the English Language Practitioners. This paper is a humble attempt to analyse the utility value of the language laboratories. It also focuses on the futility dimension of language laboratories.

The positive intention behind initiating multi-media language laboratories was to reinforce the theoretical aspects dealt with in the classroom and to provide a proper platform for the learner to enrich his communication skills. The concept of language lab assumed greater significance in the light of plethora of innovations, methods and techniques used to benefit the learner. It created a favourable ambience for the learner to practise language more effectively and efficiently.

Learners love to use the work stations in an air conditioned lab and they spend considerable time working on language software. In certain institutions highly sophisticated and expensive equipment is put to use in the laboratories. The self instructional and user friendly software with online testing and evaluation really benefits the learner. The advent of these labs made the teachers done a new role that of a facilitators. There is also a notion held that the role of the teacher is minimized as most of the software is interactive. In language lab session software is prescribed and the students are expected to browse it. It is felt that the teachers may not get ample time for one to one interaction. But both the hardware and software platforms facilitate the teacher to monitor the activities and also seek remedial measures in the event of the learner committing errors. Language software on almost all the areas of grammar, phonetics, vocabulary, conversation skills and composition is available in the market. It is developed after thorough research. Keeping in view the learners' profile and level, the Boards of Studies recommend the software. This paper examines the role of laboratories in imparting the awareness of phonetics and the essentials of spoken English.

One crucial question before the teacher (especially in professional colleges) is the iota of phonetics to be taught. Teaching of phonetics is indispensable, but determining the quantum is a big task. The situation where there are students from vernacular background is more delicate. Any attempt to dump excessive in puts may be counterproductive. It is more challenging to handle students from the Northeast and the Middle-east. During my four year stint at the Jawaharlal Nehru Technological University, I had the opportunity to teach students from Mizoram, Sikkim, Yemen and Saudi Arabia. The students come with raw expression and the MTI (Mother-tongue influence) is conspicuous and obvious. I did find the perceptible coldness in grasping the nuances of speech mechanism. It is felt that their natural expression gets victimized in pursuit of the so-called intelligibility. The excessive thrust on jargon and classification of sounds makes the learning insipid. Learner develops a kind of antipathy and he yearns to shift his focus on grammar and vocabulary thanks to language software available on phonetics. The latest software on phonetics judiciously caters to the needs of the learner. The identification of sounds is made easy through apt illustrations. In certain labs mirrors are arranged in order to enable the learner check his mode of articulation. *English Pronunciation in Use* developed by Cambridge is a value addition to the existing software. The levels of teaching are taken into consideration by the software developers. But mere browsing of software and practice of exercises may not fully equip the learner. The course instructors in the laboratory with the help of manuals can undertake the follow up activities. The multimedia lab may not provide the formal context. To test whether the sounds uttered are intelligible, it is important to conduct activities in the communication lab (a conventional lab with PA system). The real practice can be given and the genuine feedback can be obtained by planning activities in the communication lab. Language lab primarily takes care of receptive skills. But for the teaching and testing of productive skills, the role of the teacher is indispensable.

Similarly a host of items of software are available on spoken English. In fact there is proliferation of software and mushrooming of institutes of spoken English. The programmes come with a pack of activities on grammar, vocabulary, situational dialogues, comprehension, sentence formation, etc. The learner finds items like *English in Mind* (by Cambridge) very interesting. The exercises are progressively difficult. It provides number of situations for the learner and exposes him to variety of expressions. At the end of practice the learner gets definitely enriched. But it is important for the learner to get a formal context to use the language situation ally and appropriately. For this, teacher can plan post-lab activities. This will provide ample opportunity for keenly observing the errors of the learner and to take required remedial steps for improvement. However innovative and latest may be the software, if the learner is not evaluated by the teacher, the lab concept becomes futile. The use of software to some extent lessened the burden of the teacher. Effortlessly tests are generated and evaluation becomes easier. But to target the students with mixed abilities, depending totally on the software may not fetch desired results. Lab is a real asset for the teacher and the taught. Yet, dispensing with the real instruction and total dependence on software will make the process of learning mechanical. A lacuna that affects qualitative language learning is the improper synchronization between the theory and lab component. To ensure uniformity and consistency of the planned activities, they have to go simultaneously. For example, in certain institutions students are entrusted with the task of working on particular software without reinforcing the required concepts. Consequently, the lab activity becomes totally meaningless.

A more holistic approach towards the use of labs is the need of the hour. The lab has a tremendous utility value with certain limitations. The following are the constraints:

- Inadequate facilities in the lab (infrastructural)
- Availability and affordability of software (institutions can, but an individual cannot afford)
- Number of lab sessions
- Suitability of the software
- Computer illiteracy of the learner

In a nutshell, the following are the advantages of language lab:

- Learners' autonomy
- Visual experience
- Interactive software
- Online teaching and testing
- Teacher as a facilitator
- Conducive atmosphere for learning.

The judicious use of lab will certainly help the learner and the teacher. But excessive use without healthy interaction will reduce the labs to mere browsing cafes.

13

Spoken English Institutions and their Relevance

E. Vijaya Raghava

1. Introduction

Spoken is a word referred to language skills and the communication of information. Of some 3000 existing languages, large and small English is second only to Chinese in number of speakers. Communication features are: the people involved, subject matter where and when the communication is taking place and the purpose of communication. Speaking language effectively in different situations and for different purposes is the primary aim of language learners.

2. Spoken English Institutions and their Relevance

The main objective of these institutes is to impart language skills to learners and make them effective speakers. Learners approach these institutions with a specific purpose and these institutions strive a lot to meet them from time to time. They are readily accessible, adaptable and available to learners from dawn to dusk. Learners look at these institutes to get their language needs fulfilled. These institutes have a greater accountability in meeting the growing demand and challenges of language learners. They are well-equipped with study material, language labs and dedicated faculty.

3. Crazy and Demand for Spoken English

There has been much crazy and demand for spoken English over the years due to the contribution of various factors. The factors include: Impact of globalization, ample educational, employment and business opportunities across the globle, mushrooming of BPO, corporate and software companies and rapidly developing global telecommunications infrastructure, besides these it is widely used as a link language and language for correspondence in public and private sectors in our country. A graduate cannot secure a job, unless he is good at communication skills. A mother can not teach her children effectively unless she is good at English. As almost all subjects are in English language. Right from a businessman to a professional, speaking in English has become very essential. As oxygen is indispensable for our survival, so is the English language. It has become a part and parcel of our life which can not be separable. As is the usage of mother tongue at home, so is the usage of English language outside. Speaking in English has become a status symbol from an illiterate to a professional and it has become not only a status symbol but also a symbol of survival.

4. Learners' Need, Purpose and Background

Language learners approach institute with a specific purpose. Their primary objective is to attain mastery over English language and become effective speakers. Some wish to learn basic course, others advance course. Majority of the learners approach the institutes with a wish to get rid of language phobia, as they are hesitant. Though they are good at English yet they are scared to speak. Some students are good at speaking and would like to be effective speakers and their need is to learn speech skills accent, intonation and rhythm.

Learning Grammar, participating in Group discussions, and learning how to take interview skills are the purposes of some learners in addition to learning language skills such as listening, speaking, reading and writing.

It is a gigantic task for the institutions to train the learners with different backgrounds with different purposes. They are from different educational and environmental background, different family and financial background, different accent and age background besides different languages background.

Teaching these all together in the same batch is really a tremendous challenge for a teacher since their language levels are different and teacher's responsibility lies in making them understand effectively, enthusiastically and equally. Each and every learner is observed very keenly and teacher has to change his way of teaching and follow teaching techniques according to classroom situation and facial expressions of students to produce good results.

5. Learners' Views about Learning English

Learners' views on purpose, sources of learning and teacher.

When the learners are enquired about their purpose of learning English, majority of them said to get a good job, to communicate effectively and to achieve their goal through English language as it is the source to fulfill.

The best sources of learning and speaking English are: Newspaper reading, watching English news and English Channels, Speaking English at home, with friends and relatives, observing very keenly while others speak and observing others actions keenly and translating them into English immediately.

The best teacher is friendly, takes part in class as a co-learner, activates, encourages and motivates learners frequently in addition to generating a lot of examples and creating a lot of situations to speak.

6. About Institution

Victory Spoken English Institution was started in 1989 at Mehdipatnam in Hyderabad with an aim to impart language skills for academic, communication and other specific purposes, besides creating language awareness and purpose in the enthusiastic and desired language learners.

7. Objectives of the Institution

The primary objective of the Institution is to teach effectively, instill confidence and get rid of language phobia in the learners. The motto behind starting this institute is to make an illiterate a literate who courageously says after learning the course that "I too can speak English". No student is denied admission on the basis of his poor knowledge/performance in the language. Institute shoulders the responsibility that he/she makes impossible possible. Teaching language in an easy and simple methods with motherly affection, dedication and enthusiasm are the strong pillars of institution. It believes that something is better than nothing. If a student is received with motherly affection, counselled positively, taught friendly, encouraged frequently and admired timely can, of course, comes out with flying colours. This is what learners expect and institute expects.

8. Admission

Language levels of a learner are tested at the time of admission by asking the meanings of simple words, sentences and grammar contents. Learners' deficiencies, strengths and weaknesses are noted down along with purpose of learning. This facilitates the teacher to arrive at a concrete decision where to start, how to start and what methods to adopt to produce better results.

9. Course and Syllabus

Two long term courses are offered in addition to three short term courses. Two long term courses are: Basic level and advance level. Each level is for three months duration and each batch's duration is for two hours.

Three short term courses are: (a) Spoken English (Crash course), (b) Grammar, and (c) Interview skills. Each course is for 15 to 30 days duration and each batch's duration is for two hours.

Syllabus: Syllabus has been designed as per the purpose and need of the learner and it is organized in the right order. Syllabus is so easy, simple and in order that even a basic learner too can understand and gets interest to learn and practice regularly.

10. Teaching Methods

Majority of the learners are at elementary level basic ones in this institute. So the basic chapters are prepared in English and in their mother tongue (Particularly in Hindi and Telugu). Teaching is done in three stages. In the first stage it is taught in their mother tongue, second stage after the completion of the chapter, questions/sentences are asked in their mother tongue to translate them into English. In the final stage students are made to converse in that particular chapter by practising the questionnaire provided to them. The learners understand the chapter very easily as they have already learnt and practised it three times. Their confidence level goes up and they are able to produce similar and different sentences in that chapter. They get perfection by learning chapter after chapter and they are able to speak with accuracy and fluency. Gradually they can speak grammatically correct, with good vocabulary, accent and become effective speakers. Learners converse in class everyday, each learner is given five minutes time to speak on selective topics. For effective results, teacher has to make use of teaching aids such as charts, advertisements, newspapers, pictures, posters and objects of daily use. Advertisements issued by different public and private sectors are given to learners and are asked in what way they are informative, appealing and luring the customers. Discussions are held on each topic with benefits and drawbacks. Graphs, flow charts, pie charts, tree diagrams, route maps, describing processing, reporting news and discussing the subject matter of advertisement product and its visuals for effective teaching.

11. Language—Basic Skills

Language skills are taught with utmost care and devotion. The four language skills are: listening, speaking, reading and writing.

Listening: Learners learn language quickly only by listening to speech. Learners can discriminate sounds in words. Learners are made to listen to lecture attentively and are questioned frequently whether they have understood or not and asking them to reproduce the sentence again.

Speaking: Speech skills play a vital role in speaking language. Learners are taught speech sounds and production of sounds in addition to correct use of stress and intonation patterns. Learners are taught language functions, such as asking for information, giving information giving advice, seeking advice, complaining, congratulating, sympathizing and warning. Appropriate expressions of these functions are taught and made to practise for effective speaking.

Reading: Passages are made to read for information, interpretation and analyzing. Observing the learners reading skills and instruct them to comprehend them in a better manner.

Writing: Writing skills are taught to learners by explaining them how to write small sentences accurately and are encouraged to write small paragraphs on daily activities, incidents, objects, persons and places in addition to letter writing and report writing.

12. Grammar and Vocabulary

A learner who has a practical knowledge of grammar can speak more effectively than those who do not possess. The set of rules in grammar help the learner to speak and write correctly apart from producing accurate grammatical structures. The rules are taught first and then assignments applying the rules are given. Grammar is taught even in mother tongue for the better understanding of the learners.

Vocabulary: Vocabulary adds colour to speech. Appropriate words make sense. Words which occur more frequently in speech are taught to learners. Learners are advised to enhance vocabulary by families of words, objects, synonyms and antonyms, contextualization, explaining the meaning in the mother tongue and word games.

13. Assessment of Learners' Performance

Learners' performance in language is assessed by questioning/testing and following methods.

Grammar test is conducted by asking questions on grammar contents, asking the questions in the form of conversation and in the mother tongue on grammar contents.

Fluency test is conducted asking the learner general questions to answer them in stipulated time. Topic-wise questions are also put and are made to answer them. Similarly the learner is also made to ask questions on a given topic and observed how many questions can be asked by him in the prescribed time.

Effective learners test is conducted to assess learners' perfection in language. Grammar, vocabulary and accent are tested in this test. Learner is asked to produce speech sounds and is observed keenly whether he is using correct stress and intonation patterns. Learner is asked to report both newspaper events and conversation between two persons.

14. Conclusion

Spoken English institutions play the role of a facilitator, counselor and a true teacher. They lay emphasis on the development of strategies relating to the structures to their communicative functions in real life situations at an appropriate time. These institutions still strive a lot to focus on accurate production of appropriate language in communication. As the needs of the learners have changed, modified grammar patterns and functions of language only can fulfil the needs of learners for specific purposes and objectives.

14

Reading and Writing: A Case Study of Success in ESL Classroom and CBSE Board Exams

D. Murali Manohar

Introduction

English in a second language classroom situation is very scary for the students who come from rural areas with mixed economic background. The teaching that has been going on in Vidyalayas is in Hindi medium or in any regional language medium. The students are used to it and they have been getting along with the subject. It is not to criticize any teacher. But I feel it is better to share my experience with the Pedagogy teachers. I may have some influence over who may want to teach English in Direct Method. My stand on this is that English has to be taught in Direct Method not in any other method even if it were to be to an ESL classroom situation.

Objectives

The objective of teaching English in Direct Method is to build confidence in reading and writing for coping with English language in any situation especially to perform best in board exams and make them get good marks. The students are scared of the subject and are not confident enough to read and write. This paper mainly focuses on reading and writing from the examination point of view. However, one can not ignore listening and speaking. These skills were handled separately while the lessons were covered. Hence there is a brief discussion and how those skills were handled.

Review of the Situation

The school that I am talking about is Navodaya Vidyalaya, Pabra, Dist. Hisar, Haryana. The Vidyalaya is under the Navodaya Vidyalaya Samiti, Regional Office, Jaipur and headquarters being at New Delhi. The Vidyalaya is fully funded by Ministry of Human Resources Development, Govt. of India. The Vidyalaya is located in a remote village with both the mixed economic background. The Vidyalaya follows CBSE syllabus which has up to XII level. The streams offered are Arts and Sciences. The subject that I dealt was English and the classes that I taught were class XI and XII. The other two Trained Graduate Teachers were handling classes from class VI to X. The two English teachers who taught them English from class VI to X have been following Grammar Translation Method and Bilingual Method. The pass percentage was not 100 per cent and there was no question of quality result in the board exams for both X and XII classes.

I joined the Vidyalaya in the month of November, 1995. The syllabus was supposed to be completed by December end. I had a target of 100 per cent of results for class XII students. Unfortunately I could not produce 100% results in the joined year which was in the middle of the academic year. The Deputy Director came to review the results of all subjects. When came to English subject, he asked me why it was not 100 per cent. I explained the situation that I joined only in November I could not produce 100 per cent results. I did say that there was a considerable improvement as compared to the previous year's result. He was not satisfied. He warned me to pack my luggage if I did not produce 100 per cent in the next board exam. I was yet on probation.

Methodology

When I entered the classes XI and XII of Science and Arts groups, consisting of 12 and 30 respectively, with lot of pedagogy knowledge about Psychology, Sociology, Language Teaching Methods, Lesson plans, subject knowledge of

Grammar, Linguistics, and Phonetics did not work initially. I told them that I would be following Direct Method unlike Grammar Translation Method or Bilingual Method.

Listening

The students started resisting my method of teaching in English not in Grammar Translation Method or Bilingual Method. In fact some of the students were advising me to teach in Hindi. They were so used to listening to Hindi or Haryanvi. They hardly had any English either in English or in other subjects. I said nothing to do. I tried to motivate them in paying attention to the language. I followed my Teacher Training experience (product of Regional College of Education, Mysore) in introducing the difficult words by providing learning experiences. Any language learning starts with hard words. To teach the hard words in translation method or straight away giving a meaning to the word would not make them remember the meaning of the word. Thus I had to give learning experience by giving a situation and thus introducing the word and making them understand through the context. Even some of the textbooks give glossary with which the students do not remember the word in the long run. By giving situations the students are exposed to more listening to the words than getting a meaning in a short cut method. The more they listen to English language the more they are exposed to it.

Speaking

I knew that when students were made to understand in Hindi or Haryanvi and spoke most of the time in Hindi or Haryanvi, how I could change them to speak in English. While teaching, I used to ask simple questions for which they were giving me right answers in Hindi but I insisted them to give them in English let there be mistakes or speak in butler English. The aim was to make them speak right or wrong sentences. According to N. Gopalakrishnan Nair:

> English Language Teaching programmes at the school and University level have traditionally been concerned with the development of the linguistic skills of

> reading and writing. Teaching the skills of oral communication, the most important and difficult aspect of language teaching has been almost ignored. (1996: 1)

Initially they were feeling shy because it was a co-education school and naturally they had this fear. I motivated them that they were after all their classmates. Then slowly they started speaking in the class and answered in English. Very little Hindi was used in this class. The motivation part was that in all the subject classes they were taught in Hindi Medium up to class VII. Thereafter they had English Medium. My logical reason was that in all the classes they were taught in Hindi and made them think in Hindi. At least in English period, I had requested, all of them including Arts stream to speak in English, think in English, read in English, dream in English, and sleep in English. I went back to my student days of the seminars. When I had seminars I was also like them very scared to face the audience and to speak before the classmates. The class XI students had a supplementary textbook. I announced in the classroom that each one of them had to make a presentation of the lesson for ten to twenty minutes. The purpose was to make them speak before the classmates. Surprisingly they did it. Some took exactly ten minutes and some took fifteen minutes and some utilized all the twenty minutes who were above average students. They never had this kind of opportunity. It was something different for them. They had been taught English by different methods but the method I approached was totally different. I broke the myth that the Direct Method does not function. It did function very effectively.

Secondly the English teacher has to play a major role not just in classroom situation but also in other aspects such as in Morning Assembly, Mess, Reading/Study Hours, etc. Ask them to interact in English all the time at least with the English Teacher. Correct them whenever and wherever it is possible.

Reading

Then I started making them read in class. They were very reluctant. I made my speeches of how useful reading in class before all their classmates. They felt encouraged. They were not bad. They had no opportunity to read before in the class. They were provided the opportunity. English teacher is supposed to be a facilitator but not to have the attitude of show off business. Slowly they started liking reading. According to H.A. Cartledge in his essay "Reading Aloud":

> Before he becomes fluent in spontaneous conversation, a good substitute is available in the thoughts of other people, written down for him to read out. When he can read aloud intelligibly and with comprehension, he feels that he is making tangible progress, even in the most elementary stages of learning. (1967: 138)

Further Michael West opines:

> Reading aloud to the class is valuable for (1) practice in understanding correctly spoken English, (2) appreciation of literature; but unless this reading is well done, it can be of little value; it may even be boring penance to the listeners. (1967: 139)

Whenever I made them read, I used to correct their pronunciation. If necessary I used to give them few lectures on phonetics. This was one of the aspects they liked very much. There was no teacher who could teach on this aspect. Fortunately I had five semesters of exposure on phonetics and this was my favourite topic to teach at any level. I had drawn their attention to the phonemic transcription of each word in an Oxford dictionary. I carried the dictionaries to the class to demonstrate the words and how to pronounce while reading the lesson.

Writing

After completing the syllabus in Direct Method, I also conducted daily tests. I used to announce that every evening they had to write a test on each lesson. The syllabus was to read one lesson thoroughly. They were told not to read any guide or test paper as in the previous class examinations (from classes VI to X). Conducting test alone will not bring the fruits. The fruits can be eaten only if the corrections were made daily.

It was a huge task to correct same evening and give them back their scripts next day. Otherwise they would not show any interest in writing daily test. I had a great time and difficult time in correcting the scripts. At the same time my legs were pulled by many of my colleagues who used to say why take so much of pain in improving their subject, knowledge, and marks.

After the first day I found the writing was worst. The earlier situation was that the teachers used to give expected questions from the guides or test papers as the teachers were lazy in formulating questions in their own language based on the lesson. I had always liked them to give simple questions on comprehension, naming all the characters major and minor, testing them on what the important characters are, what was relationship between the characters, etc. Moreover, these questions were asked to make them feel at ease because the main characters will be known and could be answered. In a way they were motivated to read the lesson thoroughly. After the recall and recognition of questions, I used to give them application level questions by giving a statement on which they had to throw light. The application questions worked wonders. The main idea of this test was to improve their writing skills as well as their reading skills. Without reading the lessons thoroughly how can they write any answer?

Findings/Results

In the first year when I joined in the middle of the academic year, the result was not encouraging. There was a threat from the higher authorities. Having followed the above steps I could get the best results in 1996 CBSE exam standing Second Best in producing excellent results with 100 per cent result with quality marks in terms of average marks at the regional level. The region consists of States such as Haryana, Rajasthan, and Delhi. The next year that was 1997 CBSE results of my XII students had shown a spectacular and tremendous performance by both Arts and Science Stream students and broke the record in standing the best in the region with not just 100 per cent result but also quality result with highest average. One can check the records in the Vidyalaya and at the regional office which may have gone to the headquarters. Of course, I have been given merit certificates for the two consecutive years with an award from the Deputy Director, Regional Office, Navodaya Vidyalay Samiti, Jaipur.

Works Cited

Cartledge, H.A. "Reading Aloud". *E.L.T. Selections*. Ed. W.R. Lee. London: OUP, 1967. 137-39.

Nair, N. Gopalakrishnan. *Indian English Phonology: A Case Study of Malayalee English*. New Delhi: Prestige, 1996.

West, Michael. "The Technique of Reading Aloud to a Class". *E.L.T. Selections*. Ed. W.R. Lee. London: OUP, 1967. 139-42.

15

Execution of Phonetics Course—Some Observations and Suggestions

P. Hari Padma Rani

At a time when phonetics is touted as the panacea for all speech afflictions and disorders in India in general and in Andhra Pradesh in particular, it becomes necessary for us to review the role of Phonetics in affecting the speaking skills of the students. Based on my experience of teaching Phonetics for 15 years at the P.G. Level in Andhra Pradesh, this paper makes some observations and suggestions regarding the execution of the Phonetics course at the PG level. While doing so, the paper takes into account the objectives, syllabus and the evaluation process.

When we ask question, "what is the main objective of including Phonetics in the curriculum?" immediately comes the answer "it is incorporated into the curriculum because students can improve their speaking skills with the help of the theoretical inputs they gain from the course". As for the syllabus and evaluation pattern, the Phonetics in all the state universities includes either all or most of the following topics:

- The speech mechanism
- The organs of speech
- The classification and description of speech sounds: vowels and consonants
- The vowels and consonants in English

- Phonology
- The syllable
- Consonant clusters in English
- Word-Accent
- Accent and Rhythm in connected speech
- Intonation
- Phonetic transcription

A glance at the model question papers followed in such state universities as Sri Venkateswara University, Tirupati; Osmania University, Hyderabad; Andhra University, Vishakapatnam and Sri Krishndevaraya University, Anantapur show that the evaluation is completely based on a written exam. It does not include an oral component/change in the speech habits of the students on account of the phonetic course. Thus there is no evaluation system to test the realization of the objective set for the phonetic course.

Now can Phonetics really fulfill the objective set for it? Is it really crucial for teaching /learning spoken English? In the light of the high claims made for Phonetics in improving the spoken English of the students, it would only be appropriate to subject it to a close scrutiny. I must point out here that I do not in the least intend to undermine the importance of Phonetics but merely point out the subject may not be the solution for the speaking problems of the students.

I may be forgiven for using an analogy from my personal life but I find it very useful in making my point clear. My ten year old special son has no speech at all. The only sound he can articulate is something like the vowel /a/. About three years ago a well-meaning elderly lady who knew the child well advised me to teach him Sanskrit slokas. She assured me that he would pick up language easily if we taught him Sanskrit.

Needless to say, my way of teaching Phonetics to improve the spoken English of the students is akin to the advice given by the elderly lady. Phonetics, as a subject, is found interesting and enjoyable by majority of students and it can be studied for the insights it offers. But expecting the subject to fulfill such a lofty objective as this would be fallacious and untenable

Phonetics can at most help cosmetically beautify or aesthetically garnish the speaking skills of those who can already speak English to some extent at least. But it is of little use in enabling the students to speak English. I would like to quote an example here:

Majority of the girl students who came to us for pursuing their M.A. in English fail to speak any English at all even at the end of the programme in spite of having studied Phonetics. Painfully, Phonetics does not seem to come to the rescue of these girls at all. The giggle and chuckles of the squirming girls in the class while teaching them the different sounds are a clear indication of the huge gap between the spoken English they know and the English they are expected to know. Phonetics is one of the five papers the students study in their first semester at Mahila University. Last year when I had conducted the first internal test in Phonetics, 90 per cent of the students failed. When my hopes of their doing better in the Second test were also dashed, in a state of desperation, I made an announcement in the class: "I will dictate 10 sentences to you from Balasubramanian's *A Textbook of English Phonetics for Indian Students*. For every correctly written sentence I will award two marks." The sentences I gave them are these lest you should think I gave them some involved and convoluted ones: This test was conducted after Phonetics was taught and all these sentences, may be in slightly varied forms, were used by me in the course of my teaching.

1. The human articulatory system is capable of producing a variety of sounds.
2. No language has the total inventory of speech sounds.
3. The organization of sounds to form meaningful word is different in different languages.
4. Phonology deals with the selection and organization of sounds in a language.
5. No two languages have identical phonological system.
6. A phoneme is a minimal contrastive sound unit in the sound system of a language.

7. Phonetic symbols are enclosed with in slant lines when they represent the phonemes in a language.
8. Vowels are articulated with a stricture of open approximation.
9. For the articulation of most vowels some part of the tongue is the active articulator.
10. A diphthong is a vowel glide occupying a single syllable.

Can you guess the outcome? None of the twenty students could write all the ten sentences correctly. The average number of correctly written sentences was 3 with 7 as the highest and 0 as the lowest.

My intention here is not to escape my students in an unfavourable light but to draw the attention of the academia to a real situation which does not have any semblance of the ideal.

In a context like this, what the students need is not Phonetics but something more fundamental than that. It is something that would enable them to speak rather than deter them from attempting to do so. Over teaching Phonetics in our eagerness to achieve a quick cure for students' speaking inability, in fact, reinforces students' diffidence in them and can retract them from the desired goal.

Though students in general seem to like the subject for what it is, they do not seem to apply to their own speech what they learn from the Phonetics class. In order to see for myself, how far the objective of teaching Phonetics is realized, I have conducted a small scale study involving 25 post graduate students of English who have finished studying Phonetics. The study of course has many serious limitations and some of them are:

- All the students have been taught Phonetics by a single teacher, i.e. me.
- All of them are girls and most of them cannot express themselves clearly either in writing or speech.

- The study focuses only on words in isolation and does not take into account larger chunks of language.
- Each student was asked to read out around 700 words with the full awareness that reading them out is not the same as using them on their own in their speech.

There was no way by which one could make them speak in a natural and spontaneous manner. The main idea behind making them read was to see how far they apply features of accent and phonological rules they have learnt in the Phonetics course to their own pronunciation of words.

As for the words chosen for the study, *Collins Cobuild English Dictionary* (1995) based on its corpus of over 200 million word evidences, gives information about the frequency of head words. The dictionary uses five frequency bands in the form of black diamonds. The most frequent words have five black diamonds against them, the next most frequent four, and so on. The dictionary claims that the words with five and four banded frequency constitute 75 per cent of all English use. There are about 700 words in the five banded frequency and 1200 in the four banded one.

I have picked up the 700 most frequently used words in English from the *Collins Cobuild Dictionary*. Most of these words are grammar words and are monosyllabic. There are about 270 polysyllabic words I dictated all the seven hundred words to the students and asked them to transcribe them at home with the help of a dictionary and informed them that they would be required to read them the next day. The following general features have been noticed in the students' reading of the words:

- while pronouncing words beginning with weak /ə/ such as about, account, across, again and allow, almost all the students were pronouncing them with an initial /e/ sound.
- while pronouncing words like aid, again, available, eight and against they were using an extra /I/ after /ei/.

- they read most words like also, although, action, answer, any, area, army, become, begin, body, capital, carry, colour, money, etc. without stressing any syllable in a monotone.
- they pronounced certain words like event, develop, figure, hundred, letter, product, business and building with stress on the wrong syllable.
- they did not aspirate the syllables that needed aspiration.
- they had problem in getting the vowel sound correctly in words like girl, learn, sir, and word.
- they did not make /r/ mute in words like court, course, care, better, share, sure and work.
- they also had problem in pronouncing the /ɔ:/ correctly in words like law, order, fall, and form.

The students' reading of the words clearly pointed out that they have not learnt the pronunciation and the stress features of some of the most commonly used words in English. It occurred to me, while conducting the study, that given the importance of certain words in terms of their frequency of use, the Phonetics course would perhaps do better if it focused on teaching the pronunciation of all the basic words which are said to constitute "75 per cent of all English use". These words which amount to less than 2000 in number connected speech. This is likely to improve their listening comprehension as well.

Thus in addition to the topics we already have on the syllabus of Phonetics, if we can have one more topic like "Practice in the pronunciation of 2000 most frequently used words in English" the Phonetics course might become practically more useful to students.

I wanted to use humour to sensitize students towards the spoken aspects of English. Though this did not work well with my students, I am sure it will surely work in contexts where the comprehension levels of the students are higher.

16

An Observation on the Errors Made by the Customer Service Representatives in an International Call Center

Srinivasa Kumar Kolusu

ABSTRACT

The fast-growing Indian Business Process Outsourcing (BPO) industry is set to emerge as one of the biggest service providers in the world. However, due to customer dissatisfaction, several questions raised by the multinational companies about the quality of the services provided by the Indian BPO industry.

The nature of sentence construction, accent, pronunciation, and diction, the use of vocabulary, listening and reading comprehension—all pose to an American or a British customer to understand Indian English a quite challenging. In fact, it is very difficult to understand the very dialectal English (spoken by the Customer Service Representatives (CSR) by an American or a British customer in a telephonic conversation. Hence, there is an urgent need to address this problem.

The present study conducts a field study in Hyderabad by visiting a few BPOs. Data will be conducted from the primary sources such as CSRs and Trainers to know the ground level situation. Questionnaires are used for this purpose.

The collected data will be organized properly and analyzed considering grammar and pronunciation of the utterances. Based on the analysis and further interpretation of the results, necessary recommendations and suggestions will be made to make the Indian vernacular accent more globally intelligible.

Business Process Outsourcing

The drive towards reducing costs in order to raise the profit margins by the companies across the globe led to centralizing services, reducing branch offices close to the customer and taking advantage of labour costs in a location outside main business centers. Business Process Outsourcing industry permits all these activities.

Call Center

A call center is a service center with adequate telecom facilities, access to internet and wide database, which provides voice based or non-voice based services across the globe led to centralizing services, reducing branch offices close to the customer and taking advantage of labor costs in a location outside main-business centers. Business Process Outsourcing industry permits all these activities. Call centers exist in all sectors. The wide area of services provided by the call centers makes it a lucrative career with a range of opportunities.

Why India?

The large pool of English-educated and IT-educated workforce, a well-established information industry with proven record and low labor-cost has led multinational companies either to set up or outsource their business operations in India. With the opening up of the Indian economy and the advent of globalization, more and more companies from abroad are either basing or outsourcing their call center services to India, a trend started by GE when it established a call center near New Delhi in 1998.

Geographical location of India is also an advantage to India. A twelve-hour time difference with North America enables overnight delivery of services. This unique advantage helps American organization achieve true 24×7 international operations and customer service. The time zone advantage provided by India can also become a strategic enabler for many West Europe and Asia Pacific based organizations.

The commitment of the Government of India to develop world class knowledge based outsourcing industry by establishing IT and telecom infrastructure has also helped India emerge as a prominent outsourcing hub. BPOs also provide the world of career options to the millions of unemployed graduates in India. The career avenues provided by the BPOs is one of the best-suited and growing option, which even a fresh graduate can opt for.

The Problem Area

There is no doubt that Indian Business Process Outsourcing (BPO) is one of the fastest growing industries in the world. But, because of differences in pronunciation some customers are dissatisfied and questions are raised by the multinational companies about the quality of the services provided by the Indian BPO industry.

Indians do not speak the way the Americans or the British speak. They learn English as a second language. Obviously the English spoken by Indians is heavy dialectal and it is a tough task for them to understand native speaker's slang, jargon, acronyms, idioms, etc. The nature of sentence construction, accent, pronunciation, diction, the use of vocabulary, listening and reading comprehension—all pose to an American or a British customer to understand Indian English a quite challenging. In fact, it is very difficult to understand the very dialectal English (spoken by the Customer Service Representatives (CSR) by an American or a British customer in a telephonic conversation. The same problem forced Dell Inc., the largest computer seller in the world to shift its customer support service for corporate clients back to the US.

Some of the CSRs have some bad experiences with their customers. The worried customers, in general, go irate when their problems or queries are not solved in time. However, some customers feel disgusted when they couldn't understand the CSR's language. It clearly states the seriousness of the problem with the quality of the services provided by the Indian

BPO industry. Hence, there is an urgent need to address this problem.

The Need

The issue of changed ownership of English from England to America, the implications of English as an international language, the availability of a large pool of English-speaking and computer educated human resource in India and the raising doubts on the quality of service delivery by the Indian BPOs—all these led to focus on the phonological intelligibility of English language spoken by CSRs in an international call center environment.

Being the largest English speaking population, Indian BPO industry has to take the advantage and catch up to the needs of the world and drive the country towards the direction of a developed country.

Hence it is felt that there is an urgent need for theorists and practitioners to take English as international language phonology and address the problems faced by the Indian CSRs. Instead of continuing to promote the ways of describing and teaching pronunciation which have become irrelevant to the changed role of English in the multilingual world. The need of the hour is to respond quickly to the problem and solve in a realistic way.

The Objectives of the Study

- To identify the grammatical and phonological errors made by the CSRs.
- To give suitable suggestions based on the analysis of the data.

The Customer Service Representatives

Selection Process: Any graduate with good communication skills is eligible. If the candidate possess excellent communication skills, graduation is not a compulsory requirement. During the selection process candidates will be tested for oratory skills, listening comprehension, technical knowledge (computer knowledge and internet concepts) and voice and accent training.

In-house Training: Selected candidates will be given a one month in-house training covering English phonology, speeches, etiquette and culture during the first two weeks and technical and nesting training in the next two weeks. During nesting phase, trainee is allowed to barge and listen to the live calls.

The Scenario at the Operation Floor

The firm has a mix of CSRs whose experience range from less than one year to more than two years. The average call handling time is around seventeen minutes. A CSR, on an average, receives around ten to fifteen calls in an eight hour shift. They give technical support to the internet customers of the client. The basic complaints they receive are as follows:

- Not able to connect to the internet
- Not able to receive the emails
- Changing from one internet service package to another
- Ordering routers
- Internet securities
- Service level commitments
- Hardware related problems
- Network related problems
- Router installation procedure
- Browser related problems

The calls are monitored by the team leaders and voice coaches to find out the errors made by them during the conversation. Different performance evaluation tests will be conducted regularly by the firm as well as the client. Once such critical performance evaluation test is called C-Sat Test (Customer Satisfaction Test). CSRs will be evaluated on a one to ten scale. The scale between one and seven is considered as dissatisfied and eight to ten as satisfied. Other quality tests are speak clearly, Wrap Time, etc.

Data Collection

The purpose of the study is to identify the errors made by the CSR in an international call center environment. Grammar and Pronunciation are considered for the study. The field study is carried out for nine days. The first three days were spent to interact with the CSRs and to collect their personal, academic, and professional information and their experiences as a CSR. A questionnaire was prepared well before and used the same for this purpose. While preparing the questionnaire, all efforts were made to see that ambiguity is avoided and simple language is used. During these three days some of the calls were barged to listen to the live conversations between the customers and the CSRs. During this period, some of the most commonly mispronounced words, phrases and exclamatory sentences were identified. The fourth day was completely dedicated to meet the trainers and the voice coaches. I shared my observations with them. The interaction helped me to know what they teach and how they teach and to prepare a list of most commonly words, phrases and exclamatory sentences for the study.

The next five days of my field study, I barged the live calls of twenty CSRs to observe their pronunciation, spending at least ninety minutes with each representative and transcribed their utterances of the most commonly mispronounced and their representative specific utterances. Eight CSRs were considered to observe grammatical errors. An observation sheet is used for this purpose. The data was considered for mutual phonological intelligibility, with the aim of giving more comfort to the customer. Based on the results obtained, suitable recommendations were made.

Analysis of Data

Out of the thirty-two CSRs interviewed, eight were considered for grammar and seventeen for pronunciation. They are all of age between twenty and twenty-nine. All of them have done their education in English medium. Other details of the CSRs are illustrated in the graphs as follows:

Male to Female Ratio	
Male	Female
24	8
75%	25%

Details of CSRs' Mother Tongue	
Telugu	33%
Urdu	17%
Marathi	17%
Tamil	10%
Hindi	6%
Bengali	6%
English	6%
Malayalam	5%

Experience of the CSRS	
< 1 Year	26%
1 – 2 Years	48%
> 2 Years	26%

Details of CSRs' Education	
Intermediate	10%
Graduation	45%
Postgraduation/Engg.	45%

Place of Education	
City	95%
Town	5%
Village	0%

Analysis of Conversations for Grammatical Errors

Conversation 1		
Speaker	**Utterance**	**Analysis**
CSR	Since how long you have been facing this problem?	# Addition of preposition unnecessarily (as there is no use of time marker)

		#Direct question inversion error. The reason may be due to over generalization of statement forms to interrogations.

Conversation 2		
Speaker	**Utterance**	**Analysis**
CSR	Just give me a moment while I pull up your data	#Customer doesn't understand initially. #Just is an impolite and wrong expression. #Too much use of present perfect tense may have resulted in over generalization. #Please would be a polite and most appropriate expression.
CU	What?	Customer doesn't understand therefore, what?
CSR	Could you Please close the page?	#instead of Window. #Lack of technical vocabulary leads to improper use of words.

Conversation 3		
Speaker	**Utterance**	**Analysis**
CSR	I am Connecting[] to one of my colleague[]	#Omission of object pronoun. #Omission of plural marker.
CSR	Don't you find 'X' mark above the address bar	#Instead to Stop button or Red buton. #Lack of technical vocabulary.

Conversation 4		
Speaker	**Utterance**	**Analysis**
CSR	I am Connecting[] to one of my colleague[]	#Omission of object pronoun. #Omission of Plural marker.
CSR	Repeatedly uses 'so'	#A marker of imprecise, uncertain and uneducated lower class speech. #It is observed that she uses it due to lack of facility of words. #And also uses it as a gap filler when she could not take a decision related to the process or the issue. #Sometimes confuse the customer and kills the listening enjoyment.
		#Instead of Stop button or Red button. #Lack of technical vocabulary.

Conversation 5		
Speaker	**Utterance**	**Analysis**
CSR	Could you please tell me how many lights are on?	A Hindi speaker who hails from Kanpur. He did his primary education in a small town. He makes interlingual errors.
CSR	So the light is not coming on!	Connection aa gayaa?

	This system is coming?	Aa rahahai kya?
CSR	How is it?	Inversion errors.
CSR	It is up there?	

Conversation 6		
Speaker	**Utterance**	**Analysis**
CSR	(Tells the Customer) One ninety-eight point one....	#As the CSR is an engineering graduate, he is exposed to the use of words such as point, period, etc. for dot. It is an element of over generalization which can be seen in this context. The over learning of point prevents him using the appropriate word, i.e. dot. We can say this error is an idiosyncratic usage of point and period.
CU	What?	CU doesn't understand what the CSR said.
CSR	Corrects himself and utters one nine eight period, sorry one nine eight dot.	
CU	OK!	

Analysis of Some Words for Phonological Errors w.r.t. NAE

The data was considered for mutual phonological intelligibility, with the aim of giving more comfort to the customer.

General Problems Faced by the CSRs to Understand the Customer

- Customers with Spanish Accent
- Voice of the aged customers

- Heavy accent with a lot of slang
- Pronunciation varies from state to state

Specific Phonological Errors

Voiceless Plosives

Words such as Ping, package, patience, person, pleasure, power, telephone, tools, two, category, colon, computer, connect and connection are not aspirated. It indicates the non-internalization of voiceless plosives and their allophonic variations.

North American Flap or Tap

The North American /t/ takes on a unique quality for most speakers of NAE when it occurs after a vowel or an /r/ and before an unstressed syllable. They normally voice and flap any medial /t/ which occurs in words such as data, database, settings, computer, authentic, internet, opportunity, started, water, etc.

- /0/
- use of /d/ instead of /t/ in inflectional suffixes (as in asked)
- pronouncing double consonant (as in illegal)

Conclusion

The data was considered for mutual phonological intelligibility, with the aim of giving more comfort to the customer. As we know, native speaker competence is impossible to non-native speakers. However, with the awareness of our problem areas in pronunciation and proper knowledge of the native speaker's phonological norms, we will be able to advocate and implement a far more realistic to our phonological errors. Hence the solutions proposed here are to give more clues to the CSR, so that he can be more intelligible to the American customer. These clues and the conscious effort of the CSR, and by learning the language from the customer himself, will facilitate the CSR to approximate the speech of native American speaker.

It can be concluded that the small scale research will be useful to the trainers in the training programs and help the

CSRs to rectify some of their language-related problems. And in-depth study is needed to understand the language related challenges of the Indian CSRs.

References

Crystal, David. *English as a Global Language* (1997), Cambridge: Cambridge University Press.

Jenkins, Jennifer. *The Phonology of English as an International Language* (2000), Hongkong: Oxford University Press.

Richards, Jack C. *Error Analysis* (1989), New York: Longman Group Ltd.

17

Difficulties Faced by M.A. English Students in Comprehending Lectures

Anand Mahanand and *Suchismita Barik*

ABSTRACT

English is increasingly being used as a medium of instruction at various levels in our educational set-up. Though the use of English at the Secondary level is optional, at the university level its use is almost universal in India. In most universities (except a few specific language universities), the medium of instruction is English. Almost all subjects—social sciences, humanities, sciences are taught in English medium. For the students English is the second language.

At the university level, lecture method is a common mode of instructional activity. Within the field of academic study apart from other activities such as reading assignments, writing assignments, projects, lectures remain the central instructional activity. Benson calls it "the central ritual of the culture of learning" (qtd. in Flowerdew 1). Though it is an important aspect of university instruction, there has been relatively little research in this field.

In this paper we make an attempt to study the difficulties faced by university students in comprehending lectures. We have selected twenty respondents from the M.A. class of English and Foreign Languages University, Hyderabad (India) to understand the nature of their problems.

In this paper first we will understand the nature and features of university lectures then study the responses, find out ways of making lectures effective and suggest some measures for effective comprehension of lectures.

Introduction

"Lecture is considered as the setting where the subject matter of a course is explained, discussed or otherwise taken up in a meeting between lectures and students" (Mason 203). It is also defined as extended piece of discourse that is delivered by one person to a group of people. They may be extempore, talk on a topic or from an outline or detailed notes or from written notes.

Lectures can be characterized as planned, message-oriented discourse delivered by one person to a group of people. There is a minimal amount of interaction between speakers and listeners. Lectures are syntactically complex and have an academic rather than a colloquial vocabulary. They also contain the following oral features as listed by researchers:

- Redundancies
- Pauses
- Dis-fluencies
- Misspeaks
- Repetition of information

Dudley-Evans mentions different styles of lectures such as:

(a) Reading style where the speaker speaks/reads from notes.

(b) Conventional style where the speaker speaks informally, with or without notes.

(c) Rhetorical style: Where the speaker presents herself or himself as a performer.

Academic lectures can pose certain peculiar problems. They include:

Listeners don't have the same degree of control over the text as do readers, who dwell on parts of the text, skip over other parts, backtrack, etc.

- Problems posed by the sound system,
- Cognates in print may differ phonetically in ways which are hard to perceive aurally.

The listeners must recognize unit boundaries phonologically which would be marked visually in a written text.

Students should be exposed to different accents, speeds, registers and lecture styles.

General Difficulties Faced by Listeners

Now let us discuss some of the problems faced by students in general:

- A strong regional or foreign accent increases the difficulty.
- It also depends on how the lecturer approaches and conceptualizes his or her material.
- Unfamiliar material.
- New approach.
- Students may have difficulties in processing the lecture's manner of speaking—speed, pronunciation and style of discourse.
- In understanding the lecturer's reference which may be culturally specific.
- Accommodating to the educational system; learning how faculty and students interact; knowing when student apprenticeship should give way to independent expression; and understanding, how reporting and discussion reflect these educational values.

Other similar problems encountered by the students are

- Speed delivery,
- Excessive load of new terminology and concepts
- Difficulties in concentrating.

Though the above mentioned problems are discussed by many researchers, problems related to pronunciation, accents, etc. are not discussed by them as for them these problems are not serious ones in their monolinguistic educational set-up. Hence we have tried to explore these through a questionnaire here.

Specific Problems

Taking clues from the above mentioned list of problems, we wanted to know what kinds of difficulties students face at the M.A. level. We incorporated a few difficulties from the above list and added our own sets of questions to get responses on specific problems and administered the questionnaire among twenty respondents of EFL University, Hyderabad. The students are from a mixed group coming both from urban and rural, English and non-English medium backgrounds. As per the responses of these participants, the following are the important problems.

Data Interpretation

The responses that we got from our questionnaire reveal that out of 20 students, 12 are able to comprehend lectures completely. There are 8 who cannot comprehend fully, 15 students are able to identify important points and less-important points and 5 students face difficulties in identifying the main and subsidiary points. Fifteen students can identify the topic of the lecture successfully whereas few can do it sometimes depending on the particular lecturer. But we can not say that no student has any difficulty, because there are very few (2 of them) who cannot identify the topic at all. We can say that probably almost all (20) students can understand the British accent as well as Indian (intelligible) accent without much difficulty. But they say that it takes some time to be familiar with it. When it comes to the regional varieties of English, many are not comfortable with it. About the organization of the lecture, 13 students are not sure. They say some lectures are well-organized whereas some other lead to digressions. Students suggest that they need more examples to understand the content clearly. They don't like long lectures and suggest for breaks in between. Perhaps some kind of interaction in-between will be better.

From the above responses we can observe that many students can comprehend the content of their lectures to some extent. But there are more who are not sure about the content. Likewise, many students can differentiate between the main points and less important points. It is to be noted that many students face problems in understanding British accent at the initial stage. Similarly, many face problems in comprehending the regional varieties of English. So efforts have to be made to negotiate. So students have to get themselves familiarize with the accent of the target language and lecturers need to mould their pronunciation to make themselves intelligible. The need of the hour is not to concentrate on a particular variety of pronunciation but different varieties of spoken English. This is required in a context when English is acquiring the status of a global language.

Solutions

Now let us take a look at some features of effective lectures. These are the outcome of research done in the field. Flowerdew states that:

Researchers have found that effective comprehension was possible when

1. The lecturer spoke in clear standard academic English at a normal pace.
2. The course of lectures was clearly organized. Well-organized lectures and good syllabi detailed in handouts or on the blackboard increased comprehensibility.
3. The students had some background in the subject matter. Previous study of a subject often served.
4. Lecture comprehension depends on how the lecturer approached and conceptualized his or her material.

Some background knowledge, some aural comprehension do help.

A second difference of this kind is note-taking. James (1977) sees lecture comprehension as a five stage process which culminates in note-taking process; Decode, comprehend, indentify main points, decide when to record them, write quickly and clearly. As John Flowerdew mentions, Chaudron, Hansen and King also emphasize the importance of note-taking in the lecture comprehension process. Another skill related to the lecture comprehension process and not found in conversation is the ability to integrate the incoming message with information derived from other media. These other media may take the form of handouts given out at the start of the lecture, the text book which forms the basic reading for the course, or visually displaced materials presented on a blackboard, overhead projector or by some other means.

Some Recommendations of Strategies

Here are some suggestions for effective lectures.

1. Speak in clear standard academic English at a normal pace. A strong regional or foreign accent increases the difficulty unless the native language of the speaker was the same as of the listener.
2. The course of lectures needs to be clearly organized. Well-organized lectures and good syllabi detailed in handouts increases comprehensibility.
3. The students had some background in the subject matter. Previous study of a subject often serves as a "second language" that is a means of communication itself.
4. We can say in the conclusion that lectures should be able to evoke responses and of interactive nature. Above all, lecture is not just a linguistic act but also a way of establishing relationship with students. If we take care of all these aspects, we will be able to overcome some of the difficulties faced by our students.

References

Dudley-Evans, T. and Tony Johns. "Variations in the discourse patterns favoured by different disciplines and their pedagogic implications." *Academic Listening: Research Perspectives*. Ed. John Flowerdew. Cambridge: CUP, 1994. 146-58.

Flowerdew, John. *Academic Listening: Research Perspectives*. Cambridge: CUP, 1994.

James, K. "Note-taking in lectures: Problems and strategies." *English for Academic Purposes*. A.P. Cowie and J.B. Heaton (Eds.) Reading: BAAL/SELMOUS, 1977.

Jordan, R.R. *English for Academic Purposes*. Cambridge: CUP, 1997.

Mason, Abelle. "By dint of: Student and lecturer perceptions of lecture comprehensions strategies in first term graduate study." *Academic Listening: Research Perspectives*. Ed. John Flowerdew. Cambridge: CUP, 1994, 199-218.

Richards, J.C. "Listening comprehension: Approach, design, procedure." *TESOL Quarterly* 17(2) (1983): 219-39.

APPENDIX

Questionnaire

This survey is done for a research paper to know about difficulties of students in understanding university lectures. Please feel free to give your responses. Your identity will not be disclosed.

Name...............................

1. Can you decode/understand fully what has been said in the lectures?
   a. Yes______
   b. No______
   c. To some extent_____
2. Can you identify the main and the subsidiary points in a lecture?
   a. Yes______
   b. No______
   c. To some extent______
3. Can you distinguish between important points and less important points?
   a. Yes______
   b. No______
   c. So some extent_____
4. Can you identify the topic of the lecture and follow the topic development?
   a. Yes______

   b. No_____
   c. To some extent_____

5. Do you face problem in understanding the British accent?
   a. Yes____
   b. No_____
   c. Not sure_____
6. Do you face problem in understanding Indian (intelligible) accent?
   a. Yes_____
   b. No_____
   c. Not sure____
7. Do you face problem in understanding regional varieties of English?
   a. Yes______
   b. No_____
   c. Not sure_____
8. Are the lectures structured?
   a. Yes_____
   b. No_____
   c. Not sure____
9. Any suggestions you would like to give to your professor on lectures?

18

Efficacy of English Phonetics for Effective Communication—A Case Study

R. Dyvadatham

Introduction

This article presents a discussion of few issues in the teaching of pronunciation to young learners of Post Graduate students of Dravidian University, Kuppam and outlines a teaching procedure. The stress/focus is on correct pronunciation of certain commonly mispronounced words by the young learners of P.G. and an attempt is made to draw a teaching procedure. The aim is on correct pronunciation and teaching young class to speak with clarity and intelligibility.

Why do Indian Learners of English Face Difficulties in Pronunciation of Certain Sounds of English?

This is because everyone in this world learns their mother tongue during their infancy. They get plenty of exposure to the mother tongue during their infancy and then attempt to speak. When a child grows up, the knowledge of the mother tongue also grows with them.

Second language learning situation is totally different. Particularly in our schools/colleges, the students do not get enough exposure to English. They do not get enough time to listen to the language before making an attempt to use.

By the time any child whose mother tongue is not English starts learning English, he/she is about 10 years old. We start teaching English in class III and so on. We do not take into account of the children's age. We send children to kindergarten when a child is 3 years old. A child has already acquired an incredibly large amount of language habits and these are the mother tongue habits. No two languages are alike in their sound system or grammar or any other linguistics aspect. Therefore when a child starts learning English as a foreign language, there is a clash in his mind between the already acquired mother tongue habits and the new habits that he is learning to acquire. No two languages have identical sound systems.

Teaching pronunciation is fundamental to the teaching of listening and speaking. It is necessary that a second language learner should be trained to respond to a totally new sound system. The orthography of English word is phonetic and that of our Indian languages are phonetic. The students often tend to pronounce words following the spelling of words. Perhaps it may be due to the influence of their mother tongue. This results in their mispronunciation.

(a) Indian languages are syllabic, that is, we write as we speak or we read as we write. Each letter stands for one sound. But in English some letters stand for more than one sound each.

(b) Silent letters in English words also give rise to wrong pronunciation. We don't have silent letters in Indian languages.

(c) Stress, at present, in our languages is situated in our script. But in English it is not indicated in writing.

(d) In the absence of proper teaching or guidance from teachers and adequate exposure, we substitute English sounds with similar sounds learnt by us in our languages. The English language contains some unusual sounds; those are not found in our languages.

These are the reasons for Indian learners of English. They mainly face difficulties in pronunciation of certain words in English. That's why it is necessary for a speaker of English to learn the phonetics of English for effective communication.

Phonetics and Spoken English

Phonetics and spoken English are the two areas of the language which are interrelated. Phonetics is the study of the speech sounds. According to *Collins English Dictionary*, phonetics is the science concerned with the study of speech process, including the production, perception and reception of speech sounds. Spoken English comprises two aspects. One is communication and another is pronunciation. So a course in Spoken English/Effective communication in English may be either in the form of 'what to say' or in the form of 'How to say'. The first one is focused on conversation/communication and the latter one is focused on pronunciation. What to say aims to teach how to express communicative functions such as asking questions, making requests, getting things done or expressing greetings, farewells, apologies, regrets, thanks, etc. How to say deals with the way of pronouncing words, phrases and sentences. Spoken English comprises the sounds of the English language as well as the aspects of communication in social circumstances. Phonetics deals with the theoretical aspects, how these sounds are produced in speech mechanism, and the variations in the speaking of the English language dialects. It is a skill. So a lot of practice in speaking the language in different situations is necessary. That's why a good understanding of the theories of phonetics goes a long way into understanding the techniques of acquiring good spoken English.

Knowledge of Phonetic Transpiration

It avoids confusion between sound and symbol, the pronunciation of a language can be learnt more effectively and intelligibly. It is a convenient device to indicate the way in which the words of a language are pronounced, it is highly scientific and precise. It is helpful in remedial teaching of pronunciation. It is used for comparing the sound systems of different languages. It is also helpful in comparing the different aspects of the same language.

Research question: How does the knowledge of English phonetics help the student for effective communication?

The writer of the article has selected the class of P.G. students of I and II Year Dravidian University Kuppam, A.P. Each class contains 30-40 students of non–English medium category in their under graduation. Most of them have come from different faculties of B.A./B.Com./B.Sc. with different social backgrounds. No one has come from English medium background. They studied English subject in their graduation under Part–I (Telugu Hindi and English but not as an optional subject). Their official communication is very poor and also not qualitative and quantitative at the entry level. They are unable to read and speak certain words in their day-to-day life. The author of the article decided to try out the experimentation on those learners in giving the knowledge of phonetics of English especially focused on teaching of pronunciation of certain commonly mispronounced words in their speaking.

Rational for the Selection of Words

English, which is an international language, is the most widely spoken of all the languages. It is important for a foreign learner of English to learn the pronunciation of English. English is certain in its uncertainty. For instance, speakers of English cannot explain why the word "put" is pronounced in one way and "but" in another way though both words contain the "u" letter. Many non-native speakers are puzzled at the way a word has a spelling different from its pronunciation. The puzzlement is due to the fact that non-native speakers are unaware of the distinction between English 'letters' used for writing and the 'sounds' of the language which are not represented by the letters. Human beings use language in the oral form more than in the written form. Pronunciation has become the part of communication. Pronunciation and communication are inseparable. That's why every learner of English should feel that pronunciation is also important in learning a foreign language like English. Pronunciation and communication are the two sides of the same coin. Both of these are inseparable. So, a sound knowledge of phonetics of English is necessary for effective communication. Hence to teach correct pronunciation, I have selected the following words which are commonly used in our day-to-day life.

List of commonly mispronounced words

1. alien
2. air
3. broccoli
4. bomb
5. café
6. chameleon
7. charisma
8. chaos
9. dais
10. depot
11. debt
12. drought
13. elite
14. environment
15. food
16. gesture
17. genuine
18. genre
19. grotesque
20. garage
21. islands
22. iron
23. jeopardize
24. machine
25. mahout
26. panacea
27. panegyric
28. plateau
29. question
30. query
31. rapport
32. realms
33. repertoires
34. suggestion
35. subtle
36. spinach
37. sabotaged
38. tormentors
39. vehicle
40. voyage
41. wrath
42. wool
43. with
44. yatch
45. young
46. bear
47. burg
48. beer
49. disease
50. leisure
51. viscount
52. psychology
53. sachet
54. poor
55. parent
56. dumb
57. ring
58. curve
59. alimony
60. bouquet

Methodology

Before commencing the experiment the author prepared a questionnaire for the students and extracted some valuable information with regard to the speaking skill or effective communication. The questionnaire contains 15-20 questions related to the speaking of English effectively. Next, the experimenter prepared a list of some (roughly 60) commonly mispronounced words for the conduct of experiment. The teaching of pronunciation with the help of phonetics of English was conducted for a period of 30 days from 01-09-2009 to 30-09-2009. The tryout was experimented in the following aspects of phonetics of English.

1. Introduction
2. Classification of sounds

3. Consonants and Vowels
4. Phonetic Transcription
5. Syllable and Syllabification
6. Stress/accent
7. Weak forms and strong forms
8. Intonation
9. Rules of pronunciation

Finally, a lot of practice on phonetic transcription of words was given with help of a good dictionary namely the *English Pronouncing Dictionary* (15th edn.) by Daniel Jones.

At the end of the experiment, i.e. 30th day, once again all the students were undergone for recording the pronunciation of some commonly mispronounced words what they have already uttered and recorded on the very first day of the experiment. Then the experimenter compared the first day recordings and the last day recording of 30-40 P.G. students' that the way they have uttered.

Administration of the Experiment

The experiment was done for a period of 30 days in a class of 30-40 students of P.G., D.U. Kuppam. Keeping the importance of English phonetics, I recorded the initial pronunciation of certain commonly mispronounced words by the group of 30-40 students at the beginning of my experiment. I called this group as pre-training/pre-experiment group. Now I would like to play their pronunciation here. Please listen carefully.

From the 2nd day onwards, I started introducing the English consonants and vowels. The sounds were presented orally and the phonetic symbols were written on the black-board with examples. Then the students were asked to repeat the sounds in words after the teacher first in unison and then individually. Intensive practice was given in those sounds and phonemic contracts that the students found difficult. The areas of students' difficulty was identified while I was recording their speech. Everyday 5-6 words out of 60 were given intensive practice how to pronounce correctly, clear articulation of sound, correct distribution of English vowels, consonants and consonant clusters, correct vowel length weakening of vowels in unstressed syllables and acquisition of /eI/ are some of the items which could be chosen for specific practice in the classrooms, since, these are important for intelligibility and acceptability of Indian English at the national and international levels.

Everyday I used to teach 45-50 minutes, one aspect of English phonetics as mentioned above along with the practice of 5-6 words. Then the students showed confidence in the use of isolated sounds in various contexts. They could be guided towards a more complete use of sound in polysyllabic words, short and then long utterances.

Finally, the last day (30th day) of my experiment, I once again recorded the pronunciation of 30-40 students of P.G., Dravidian University, Kuppam.

Analysis of the Experiment

The investigator analyzed the recording of the learners pronunciation of certain commonly mis-pronounced words on the first day and the last days of the experiment, i.e. after 30 days practical teaching of phonetics of English.

After the completion of my experiment of "Efficacy of English Phonetics for Effective Communication", I analysed the data through questionnaires, recording of pre-training and post-training and drawn to conclusions as given below. The tryout of individualized pronunciations of words is tested at two levels such as pre-training and post-training after a period of 30 days theory-cum-practice classes. The findings of the individuals pronunciation of the students recorded are of the following:

Pre-training/Pre-experiments	Post-training/Post-experiments
1. 30-40 students' speech was recorded by using certain commonly mis-pronounced words.	1. 30-40 students speech was recorded using certain commonly mispronounced words used on the first day (same words).

2. First day speech/utterance once was not clear and audible.	2. The last day speech/ utterance was very clear, audible and intelligible.
3. Only 2-3 students' pronunciation was some what better.	3. After 30 day's rigorous practice of English Phonetics almost all students were able to pronounce those 60 words correctly.
4. 15 students were very weak in pronouncing those words. Especially they used to pronounce the words by looking at the spelling.	4. After the training 15 students are very strong (confident) in pronouncing the words correctly.
5. 10 students were somewhat good in pronouncing certain words.	5. After the training, 10 students have become perfect in pronouncing certain words.

The following are some of the possible reasons to improve their skill of pronunciation:

1. Majority of the students of Dravidian University have come from Rural Background.
2. Lack of theoretical and practical knowledge of English Phonetics.
3. Students showed more interest in learning the pronunciation of some commonly mispronounced words because they would like to use those words in their day-to-day life.
4. Pupils were very happy towards the end of my experiment. They requested me to take some more classes on English pronunciation.
5. Pupils identified/recognized the efficacy of English phonetics for effective communication after the completion of post experiment.

6. It is necessary for an English learner to have an adequate knowledge of phonetics to be able to correct his/her mistakes in pronunciation.
7. To teach English Phonetics, the teacher of English should be trained.

Observation

1. Out of 40 students, 30 students are able to communicate effectively.
2. Out of 60 words, 40 words are pronounced correctly and accurately.
3. Out of 40 students, 20 students have learnt the average way of pronunciation.
4. The quality of the pronunciation of those students was more effective after introducing the knowledge of phonetics of English practically.
5. Students, questionnaire reveals that almost all the students are bilingual, i.e. their mother tongue is Telugu/Tamil/Kannada.
6. Students are expected proper training in practicing the pronunciation of English words, sentences with proper stress.

Findings, Conclusion and Suggestions

1. It can be seen from the present case study that the teaching of English phonetics for effective communication still has tremendous relevance. As a vast majority of students are strongly motivated to learn it for educational and employment purposes especially to get jobs in call centers and also in medical transcription courses. An awareness of the changing needs of our students in the last two or three decades, is manifest in the changed syllabus, evaluation patterns and pedagogic practices. However, there exists a number of lacunas in all this areas. It is hoped that this study has successfully adumbrated their ends pertaining to materials,

methods and modes of evaluation, which need to be suitably adapted, suggested to strengthen these areas.

2. English Language Teaching should follow approaches that lay stress on oral communication abilities.
3. English's syllable structure happened to be a problem for the entire student's pronunciation. At the time of testing student's articulation, there is not a single student who has pronounced the words without a single mistake, very few have been able to pronounce rightly.
4. Remedial measures should be included while teaching pronunciation. The weak areas should be diagnosed and corrected. Certain items are sure to be common for all language teaching purposes. They are word stress, sentence stress and intonation.
5. English phonetics and the sound system should be introduced right at the intermediate level. So that by the end of their graduation they will be able to acquire enough proficiency in the use of spoken English. Here correctness is more important than fluency.
6. Constant exposure to the spoken language should be provided.
7. Teacher should be trained in teaching English pronunciation. The teacher should focus on the problem area; teacher listens to the pronunciation of items containing the target sounds.

The present study may be considered as an attempt at making out a case for imparting English phonetics for effective communication to the student of Dravidian University, Kuppam, those who come from rural colleges and provide a foundation for more extensive scrutiny and study of English phonetics by the rural and urban students.

It is also hoped that the users of dictionaries learn and understand not only the meanings of lexical items but also their pronunciation.

1. Dravidian Languages are Phonetic, i.e. we write as we speak or we read as we write. Each letter stands for one sound some letters stand for more than one sound.
2. There are some silent letter words in English. That's why they fail in speaking the words with correct pronunciation. But we do not have silent letters in our Indian languages.
3. Stress at present in our languages is situated in our script. But in English it is indicated in writing.
4. Students are unable to speak those words because of inadequate exposure.
5. In the absence of proper teaching or guidance from the teachers and adequate exposure substitute English sounds with similar sounds learned by them in their languages.

References

Balasubramaniyam, T. *An Introduction to English Phonetics for Indian Learners*. New Delhi: Macmillan.

Bansal, R.K. *An Outline of English Phonetics* (1971). Bombay: OUP.

David, Abercrombe. *Elements of General Phonetics* (1967). Edinburgh: Edinburgh University Press.

Dhameeja, P.V. and P.V. Sethi. *A Course in Phonetics and Spoken English* (1989). Chennai: Tata McGraw Hills.

Focus on Pronunciation (2004). New Delhi: Prentice Hall of India.

Gimsion, A.C. *An Introduction to the Pronunciation of English*: Revised by Sasam Ramsacram.

John, Leaver. *Principles of Phonetics* (1994). Cambridge: CUP.

Jones, Daniel. *An Outline of English Phonetics* (1956). (19th Edn Cambridge: CUP.

——. *The Pronunciation of English* (1963). Cambridge: CUP.

——. *English Pronouncing Dictionary* (1997). London ELBS.

O'Connor, J.D. *Better English Pronunciation* (1980). Cambridge: CUP.

Roach, Peter. *English Phonetics and Phonology: A Practical Course* (3rd edn) (2000). Cambridge: CUP.

Sasikumar, P.V. and P.V. Dhamija. *Spoken English* (1994). Chennai: Tata McGraw Hills.

Sasikumar, V.P., P. Kirnmay and Geetha Rajeevan. *A Course in Listening and Speaking*, Vols. I & II (2005). Bangalore: Foundations.

19

English and Telugu Sound Systems: A Comparative Study

B. Bhujanga Reddy

An Introduction

yadyapi bahunaadhiiSe tathaapi paTha putra vyaakaraNam,

swajanah Śwajanoo maa bhuut sakalam Śakalam sakrut Śakrut.

In this stanza, a father told his son that "Though you did not study much, you must study grammar to avoid the mispronunciation of swajanah (relatives) as Śwajanah (lower caste people or untouchables), sakalam (whole) as Śakalam (part) and sakrut (often) as Śakrut (night soil). The author explained in this stanza the importance of phonetics—which is a part of grammar—in learning one's mother tongue. Phonetics has much more importance in the foreign language teaching and learning especially language like English which has the un-Phonetic pronunciation and spelling system.

What Happens if We Mispronounce a Word?

In the stanza quoted above, the author also gives the result of the mispronunciation that is misunderstanding, or miscommunication. Sometimes it may give a derogatory sense also.

A Practical Example

Two years ago, I taught Telugu to a Japanese student. One day, by the time I came to her class one of my colleagues was asking her that "Who is your teacher?" She said Dr. Bhujanga Reddy "gaadu". We laughed a lot. Then my colleague told her that you should not say "gaadu". It is a derogatory affix. Then I said to her that you say "gaaru" not "gaadu". Then she tried to pronounce it but failed. I repeated gaaru three more times but she could not pronounce it correctly. Then I asked her "What is the problem?" She told me that "We don't have that sound in our language."

Aims of the Paper

The aim of this paper is to find out the problems involved in teaching and learning the English language sounds by the comparison of the sound systems of English and Telugu. This comparison is useful to the teachers of English language in the preparation of textbooks and tests. Generally, no two languages have the same number of sounds. If two languages have the same number of sounds, they may not have similar sounds. If they have the similar sounds, they may not have the same sequence and distribution of sounds in words. In this situation the comparative study of two languages may come to handy to the teachers and learners of English Language.

Limitations of the Paper

This paper compares only the Standard Telugu sounds which are described by the Djordge Kostic, Alokananda Mitter and Bh. Krisnamurti (1977) with the sounds of the Standard British English which are given in the *Oxford Learners Dictionary* (2005). And it is also limited only to the segmental phonemes leaving the supra-segmental phonemes like stress and intonation. Only the differences between English and Telugu sound systems will be highlighted, because differences only create the problems in foreign language learning.

1. Comparison of the English and Telugu Vowel Sounds

In English and Telugu languages no word exists without a vowel sound.

Some persons may show the English word 'rhythm' (by the influence of spelling) as a vowelless word, but it is not correct, because the letter 'y' in this word will be pronounced as vowel sound /I/. We cannot pronounce any word without a vowel sound.

(a) Number of vowel sounds in English

Pure vowels: [ɪ, i:, e, æ, a:, ə, ɜ:, ʌ, ɒ, ɔ:, ʊ, u:]

Diphthongs: [eɪ, aɪ, ɔɪ, əʊ, aʊ, ɪə, eə, ʊə]

(b) Number of vowel sounds in Telugu

Pure vowels: [a, a:, ɪ, i:, ʊ, u:, e, e:, o., o:]

Diphthongs: [aɪ:, aʊ]

There are 20 vowel sounds in English out of which 12 are pure vowels and 8 are diphthongs. Telugu has only 12 vowels including two diphthongs. Six pure vowels [æ, ə, ɜ:, ʌ, ɒ, ɔ:] and 6 diphthongs [eɪ, ɔɪ, oʊ, ɪə, eə, ʊə] of English do not exist in Telugu. But we can hear the four vowel sounds [æ, æ: and ɔ, ɔ:] as allophones of [e, e:, o, o:] in the following one of the Telugu word pairs. (a) [meTTu] (step) (b) [m æ TTa] (dry land) (c) [me:ku] (nail) (d) [mæ:ka] (e) (goat) (f) [oke:] (only one) (g) [ɔka] (one). [ko:Ti] (crore) (h) [k ɔ: Ta] (fort). In these pairs of words the second words have the allophonic sounds of [e, e: o, o:] i.e. [æ, æ: and ɔ, ɔ:] when followed by a consonant and a vowel sound [a] (Theodore 1966: xxi).

(c) Sequence of vowel sounds

Two vowel sounds can occur side by side within a single word in English as in skiing [ski:iŋ] and being [bi:iŋ]. In Telugu it does not.

(d) Distribution of vowel sounds

(e) Representation of the vowel sounds

In some words of English the vowel sounds will be represented by consonant letters, for example, rhythm. In this word the first vowel sound [I] is represented by a consonant letter—y. And in the same word the second vowel [ə] is not represented at all.

2. Comparison of the English and Telugu Consonants

J.D. O'Connor (1972: 32) pointed out one interesting observation about the consonants of English. He opines that if we delete all the vowels of a sentence, still we can understand it. But if we delete all the consonants of a sentence, we can not make out it. So if the vowels you use are imperfect it will not prevent you from being understood, but if the consonants are imperfect there will be a great risk of misunderstanding. This is true in Telugu language too. It may be true in most of the other languages as well.

(a) Number of consonant sounds

There are 24 distinctive consonant sounds in English. The distinctive consonant sounds of English which are absent in Telugu are: [t, d, f, v, θ, ð, z, ʒ]. The English consonant sounds [t, d] are different from Telugu t, d and T, D. The English consonants /t/, /d/ are alveolar plosives, whereas the Telugu /t/, /d/ are dental plosives and T, D are post alveolar plosives. (Djordje Kostic 1977: 110-114). Telugu speakers do not face much problem in learning the English /t/ and /d/ since these two sounds are slightly differed in pronunciation with Telugu sounds. But the English speakers do not pronounce the Telugu dental plosives correctly, because they do not have these sounds in their language. They pronounce the Telugu voiceless dental plosive /t/ as alveolar plosive /t/. That's why they pronounce the name of our language as [Telugu]. Telugu illiterate speakers pronounce the English voiceless labio-dental fricative /f/ as bilabial plosive /p/ in the word [a:pi:su] for office]. Literate speakers pronounce it with /f/ [a:fi:s] only. Because of the influence of English /f/ sound, the Telugu voiceless bilabial aspirated plosive [ph] is now being pronounced as /f/ : [falitam] for phalitam (result).

The most problematic consonant sounds of English even for educated speakers of Telugu are: /θ/ and /ð/. They do not pronounce these sounds accurately. They substitute either t or th for English /θ/ as in earth [ert] and think [thiŋk]. Some speakers may pronounce the latter word with [t]. But in writing most of the Telugu speakers use either [t] or [th] for English /θ/. In the same way Telugu speakers substitute both in writing and speaking either [t] or [d] for English /ð/ as in smooth [smu:ð] and this [ðis]. The English consonant sound [z] is pronounced by Telugu speakers in the word initial position as /dʒ/: /dʒu:/ for zoo and /dʒiə:rəʊ/ for zero, but they pronounce it in the word medial and word final positions as /s/: [ka:smetic] for cosmetic [de:s] for days. Sometimes it leads to miscommunication: lazy and lacy. As there is no symbol for this sound in Telugu they use /dʒ/ in writing also. The /ʒ/ sounds also new to the Telugu speakers. So they substitute /dʒ/ both in speaking and writing.

The distinctive consonant sounds which are absent in English are: [gh, tʃh, dʒh, T, D, Dh, N, t, th, d, dh, bh, Ś, L].

The English speakers face difficulty in pronouncing the retroflex nasal and lateral approximant sounds of Telugu. Because they do not have these sounds in their language.

(b) Sequence of consonant sounds

I. The sequence of consonant clusters

The cluster sounds will occur in both English and Telugu languages as in street (English), [stree] (woman) in (Telugu). But their combinations and distribution may vary. Farb, Peter (1975: 298, 299) told some interesting facts about the English language syllable formation. His words go like this: Phonemes are like chemical elements in that they combine only with certain other elements. Combination of phonemes form syllables, but the kinds of possible syllables vary greatly from one language to another. *Slip* is an English word, but *slin* is not, even though it could be, because it follows the rules for the forming English syllables. Nothing in the sound system of English prevents the formation of the word *slin*. On the other hand, *tlip* is not an English word and it can never be one, because no native English word begins with the combination *tl*, even though this sequence of consonants is common in some other languages. On the other hand, English language encourages the clustering of consonants more than many languages do, such as the tongue twisting /mpsd/ in the word "glimpsed". Rules for the creation of a single-syllable English word have been stated in an ingenious formula by Benjamin Lee Whorf. Each of the terms in Whorf's formula is numbered 1 through 15. According to his sixth term, the consonants /k/, /l/ and /p/ either may begin a word alone or may be preceded by /s/, but if they are followed by a consonant, that consonant must be /r/ (thus forming such words as *crew* and *screw*, *train* and *strain*). The /sk/ combination may also be followed by /w/ (as in the word spelled *squash*) and the /sp/ by /l/ as in *split*)

(For other rules see Farb, Peter 1975: 302, 303). Most of the educated Telugu speakers declusterize the English words which have the cluster sounds by adding a vowel sound. For example, [warald] world; [warest] worst.

II. *Geminated consonant sounds*

There are no double consonant sounds in English, except the words like unknown [ʌnnəʊn], whereas in Telugu they are very much used: for example, [akka] sister, and [anna] brother, etc. By the influence of their mother tongue Telugu speakers usually use double the consonant sounds wherever they see the double consonant letters of English. For instance: [giddi] for giddy; [rʌbbər] for rubber; [dʌbbiŋ] for dubbing, [pʌppi] for puppy, etc.

(c) Distribution of consonant sounds

The two nasal sounds /m/ and /n/ can occur in the beginning, middle and final positions of the words in both the English and Telugu languages. No word begins with the nasal sound /ŋ/ in English and Telugu. The retroflex nasal /n/ also does not occur in word initially in Telugu. The palatal, velar nasals do occur only in the word medial position in Telugu; retroflex nasal and retroflex lateral approximant (l) do occur only in the word medial and word final positions.

(d) Representation of the consonant sounds

Generally, learners of English will depend upon the grammar books and other printed materials of that language. This printed letters do not give much information about the pronunciation of the sounds including stress, tone and intonation. By seeing the printed words we could not find out which letter is silent in which word of the English. Moreover, the same letter may represent more than one sound. For example, the letter 'o' represents six different sounds in a single sentence: The women do not pronounce words properly. In this sentence the letter 'o' suggests /I/, /u:/, /ɔ:/, /ə/, /ɜ:/, /ɒ/. The single letter may represent more than one sound in a single word also. For example, take the word capacity. In this word 'c' is pronounced in two ways: /k/ and /s/. In English it is also possible that 14 different spellings may represent the single sound. The single sound /sh/ is represented by 14 different spellings in the following words: *sh*oe, *s*ugar, i*ss*ue, man*si*on, mi*ssi*on, na*ti*on, suspi*ci*on, o*ce*an, con*sci*ous, *ch*aperon, *sch*ist, fu*chs*ia, obno*xi*ous. How can we identify the pronunciation of the sound /sh/ in these words? In some words the consonant sound /w/ of English is represented by a vowel letter as in: one /wʌn/, quick /kwik/. In some other words the consonant sound /j/ of English is represented by a vowel letter 'u': unique /jun:k/, union /ju:nion/. It is interesting to note the English spelling system that a single vowel letter can represent a triphthong. For example, wire /waiə(r)/.

Conclusion

I conclude this paper with the remarks of Robert Lado. He opines that "The teacher of foreign languages may wonder why he has to go through the painful business of comparing languages. Is it not his responsibility simply to teach a foreign language? Is it not enough that he should know that foreign language?

We assume that the student who comes in contact with a foreign language will find some features of it quite easy and others extremely difficult. Those elements that are similar to his native language will be simple for him, and those elements that are different will be difficult. The teacher who has made a comparison of the foreign language with the native language of the students will know better what the real learning problems are and can better provide for teaching them. He gains an insight into the linguistic problems involved that cannot easily be achieved otherwise.

References

Farb, Peter. *Word Play: What Happens When People Talk*. New York: Bantam, 1975.

Kostic, Djordje, Alokananda Mitter and Bh. Krishnamurti. *A Short Outline of Telugu Phonetics*. Culcutta: Indian Statistical Institute, 1977.

Lado, Robert. *Linguistics Across Cultures*. Ann Arbor: The University of Michigan Press, 1961 (Fourth printing).

McIntosh, Colin and Joanna Turnbull, eds. *Oxford Advanced Learner's Dictionary of Current English*. Oxford: Oxford University Press, (Seventh edition) 2005.

O'Connor, J.D. *Better English Pronunciation*. London: Cambridge University Press, 1970.

Theodore, B. *Better English Pronunciation of Commonly Mispronounced Words* (English-Telugu). Narsapur: Mrs. B.M.J. Theodore, 1966.

20

The Native Speaker no Longer Rules!

Sridhar Maisa

Introduction

The importance of communication across the cultures and nations has increased exponentially in the last ten years. Ecological and technological developments have contributed towards breaking down the barriers of language communication wherein people all over the world have come to share information and exchange ideas in English. The emergence of Internet is another important contributing factor for the development of English communication across cultures and nations. Globalization brought an intense competition among the internationally reputed business firms. Consequently, the need for effective communication has grown beyond expectations. Thus, an integrated approach for communication has become essential to the success of an individual or organization.

Widdowson (1994) so forcefully argues, English is no longer the property of its native speakers. In this globalised world every individual's English varies due to multidialectal and multilingual backgrounds. To maintain a standard English is a big challenge to non-native speakers of English. We have our own pronunciation with mother tongue influence. To maintain a neutral accent we definitely need training. Non-native speakers English tend to carry over the intonation and phonemic inventory from their mother tongues into their

English speech. The stress, rhythm and intonation were mentioned as major areas of learner's difficulty, Burgers and Spencers (2000) proved in their survey, over perception and production of individual sounds.

Kachru (1982) described six fallacies about the users of English across cultures. According to Kachru his six fallacy diversity and variation in English are indicators of linguistic decay.

The possible solutions for questions on pronunciation norms and modes of teaching are first we attempt to establish some sort of simplified, neutral, universal pronunciation variety, intelligible and acceptable to both native and non-native speakers of English. The second and potentially more promising approach to solve the conflict is that teaching generalized norms according to individual learners need and choice rather than a narrow focus on a standard British or American accent.

Intelligibility in EIL (English as International Language) it is necessary to maintain a balance between the segmental and supra-segmental in teaching. The areas which have greatest influence on intelligibility in EIL, i.e. certain segmental, nuclear stress and effective use of articulatory setting, to the extent that it underpins the first two areas (Dalton and Seidlhofer 1994: 142). There is a lot of influence of our mother tongues on English. David Crystal's (1969) tentative prediction is correct, English may be moving towards the syllable-timed end of the stress/syllable timing continuum, under the influence of other world languages.

Difference between American English and British English

The most prestigious accent in the United Kingdom is referred to as 'RP' as 'BBC' English or 'Standard English'. It refers to the accent of educated speakers in the entire country. It is characteristic of the upper and the upper-middle class people, barristers, diplomats, etc., it excludes the accents of the masses in the rural areas.

There is no such accent in the U.S., a local accent in the country can be recognized only in the east or the south.

'General American' is the term commonly employed for the majority of the American accents (which do not show marked eastern or southern characteristics), including both the northern speech of the Hudsonvally and upstate New York and the midland speech of Pennsylvania (Wells 1982).

Thus, General American is by no means a uniform accent. The term is generally used for an American accent without marked regional characteristics. It is also sometimes referred to as 'Network English' as it is most acceptable on the television networks covering the whole of the United States. The American English is chiefly distinguished from the British English by its emphatic expressive character. On comparing the pronunciation of particular words, it is found that the two accents are similar in many respects. For example, the vowel /i:/ is common to both the accents. That is to say, wherever RP has an /i:/, General American has a corresponding /i:/ too and vice-versa. The words such as key, clean, need, etc. are pronounced like in both the varieties of English. Likewise, the diphthong /aɪ/ is the same in RP as well as in General American. It is used in words like ripe, arrive, height, try, etc.

In some cases, the American pronunciation shows certain well-marked differences from the British pronunciation. Take, for instance, the words like hot, pot, shop, etc. Here in RP /ɒ/ corresponds either to the General American /ɑ:/, but in words like cough and Boston, etc., it corresponds either to the General American /ɔ/ or /ɑ:/. To put it differently, in stop, hot, pot, etc., General American /ɑ/ corresponds to RP /ɒ/, but in father, psalm, etc., it corresponds to RP /a:/.

The three centering diphthongs of RP /Iə/, /eə/, /ʊə/ are not available in General American instead phonetic, [/ɪə/, /eə/, /ʊə/] are found as allophones of (/I/, /e/, /u/). Similarly, the diphthong /aʊ/ in RP is replaced by our /oʊ/ in General American, which has rounded initial vowel instead schwa /ə/. Some examples are:

Word	**RP**	**Gen.Am.**
Goat	/gəʊt/	/goʊt/
Boat	/bəʊt/	/boʊt/
Foam	/fəʊm/	/foʊm/
Foe	/fəʊ/	/foʊ/

Another notable difference between RP and General American lies in the quality of /ʌ/ as in words like sun, cut, etc. In RP this vowel is more open than the corresponding one in General American and is produced by holding the jaw in slightly lower position and the tongue is somewhat more advanced, thus giving it a quality similar to that of the vowel /a:/.

Finally, RP diphthong /ɪə/ corresponds to the General American /ɪɹ/. Some examples are:

Word	**RP**	**Gen.Am**
Beer	/bɪə/	/b ɪɹ/
Fear	/fɪə/	/f ɪɹ/
Near	/nɪə/	/n ɪɹ/

Besides these main differences, there are minor differences too. For example, in the case of the word tomato, RP has /a:/ in the second syllable as against /ɑ/ in General American:

Word	**RP**	**Gen.Am**
Tomato	/təma:t əʊ/	/təmɑtoʊ/

Another important difference concerning individual words pertaining to the words been and leisure. In RP, it is pronounced in its strong form in the same as "bean" while in General American it is pronounced like "bin". As for leisure, General American has a long vowel /i:/ and RP has /ɛ/ in its first syllable.

In respect of the consonants, there is a notable difference between two varieties of English. The lateral approximant /ɫ/ is dark (velarised) in General American and clear in RP intervocalic positions, for example:

Word	**RP**	**Gen.Am**
Jelly	/dʒe lI/	/ dʒe li:/
Pillow	/pIl əʊ/	/pI ɫoʊ/

An important difference consists in the realization of /t/ in the intervocalic positions. Unlike RP, General American usually has a voiced top /ʔ/ in the intervocalic positions. RP /t/ remains voiceless in all environments.

Word	RP	Gen.Am
Letter	/letə/	/leəʔ/
Putting	/putɪŋ/	/p ʊʔɪŋ/
Writer	/raItər/	/raɪʔə/
Waiting	/weItIŋ/	/weIʔIŋ/

The most important difference between American and British pronunciation lies in the treatment of the approximant /r/. In RP, the approximant /r/ is subjected to a severe phonotactic on straight; it can occur only before the vowel. In General American, on the other hand, /r/ is not subject to any such constraint. Thus where General American has /r/ followed by a consonant, RP lacks it. For example:

Word	RP	Gen.Am
Sharp	/ʃa:p/	/ʃa:rp/

Whereas General American permits the word final /r/, RP does not unless the next word that closely follows begins with a vowel:

Word	RP	Gen.Am
Car	/ka(r)/	/ka:r/
War	/w ɔ(r)/	/wɔ:r/
Beer	/bIə(r)/	/bIr/
Pure	/pjʊə(r)/	/pjʊər/

As there are many Indian languages, their influence on English hampers general intelligibility. This influence is normally called Mother Tongue Influence (MTI). Universities, colleges and multinational companies are working towards accent neutralization so that English of the Indian students becomes globally intelligible. For example, when an employee working for a multinational company interacts with a person from another part of the world, it is important that his accent is neutral and intelligible so that there will be an effective communication.

Summary

As the important of communication increased exponentially across the cultures and nations in the last decade, economic and technological developments have contributed towards breaking down the barriers of language communication wherein people all over the world have come to share information and exchange ideas in English. As there are fewer barriers to communication, consequently, the need for effective communication has grown beyond expectations. Thus an integrated approach communication has become essential to the success of an individual or an organization. English is no longer the property of its native speakers, in this globalised world every individual's English varies due to multidialectal and multilingual backgrounds. The stress, rhythm and intonation were mentioned as major areas of learner's difficulty. Although we have different varieties and dialects of English, following a particular variety is a choice of individuals and people.

Works Cited

Crystal, David (1969). *Prosodic Systems and Intonation in English.* Cambridge: Cambridge University Press.

Kachru, Braj B. (1982). *The Other Tongue: English Across Cultures.* Chicago: University of Illinois Press.

Seidlhofer, Barbara (ed.) (2003). Controversies in Applied Linguistics. Oxford: Oxford University Press.

Wells, J.C. (1982). *Accents of English: An Introduction.* Cambridge: Cambridge University Press.

Widdowson, Henry G. (1994). "The Ownership of English". *TESOL Quarterly*, 28/2, 377-89.

21

English Pronunciation and Spelling: Mysteries and Revelations

Panchanan Mohanty

Nothing is perfect in this world. If things were perfect, we would have reached the plateau in search of knowledge and there would have not been any scope to hold such a seminar. At the end of each seminar, we realize that a lot of things have been left for the future. Imperfection is the inherent property of languages because they evolve on the earth, not in the heaven. With this initial note, I should mention that this seminar is very important. I would like to quote some statistics here.

Studies in Second Language Acquisition journal, a highly reputed and an international journal has published almost 200 articles for a period of ten years out of which only 12 to 15 articles are in the area of Phonetics and Phonology and the remaining 185 to 188 articles are in the area of grammar and semantics. This means Phonetics and Phonology are neglected in language teaching and learning. A possible reason could be that Phonetics and Phonology are difficult to master because we get used to speak our mother tongues in a particular way. Therefore, when we start learning a second language it is difficult to unlearn the mother tongue speech-habits; hence, it becomes difficult for us to acquire the Phonetics and Phonology of the target language. This could be one of the major reasons that creates serious problems in learning to speak another language.

The other point I want to mention is that when we are talking about grammar, we should know which grammar we are dealing with and also define what grammar is. For me, grammar is in the mind of the speaker and the learner of a language. It is not in any book. Language is a rule-governed behaviour. Every aspect of a language, be it spelling, pronunciation, syntax or semantics, is rule-governed. We cannot speak to one another unless we share the same set of rules. That is why, the job of a grammarian is to discover these rules and record them in a book called 'grammar book'. If a grammarian does that, he/she is a good grammarian. If one does not do it, he/she is a bad grammarian. From this point of view Wren and Martin may not be a good grammar.

Again, the other point that I want to emphasize here is that grammar is not a monolithic structure. It is not a point; it is a spectrum. There are variations in a language which you all know. For example, with reference to Telugu, we do not know for sure what Standard Telugu is. If we look at the Telugu newspapers such as *Vartha, Andhra Prabha, Andhra Jyothi,* etc. we will see that the language they use is not the same. There are differences and the same is true in the case of English. You must have heard people talking about consonants and vowels of British English. But we would find that there are quite a number of other dialects spoken in England itself. Every dialect has a life and it is a language on its own. Of course, it may not be a prestigious variety and that is why we talk about standard and non-standard Englishes.

Coming back to the topic of the seminar, in any discussion on Spoken English people usually talk about Received Pronunciation (RP). I am glad that I did not hear anybody referring to RP yesterday and today. In fact, nobody in India speaks the so-called RP. This variety of English is not very important for us. It was Daniel Jones who established and popularized RP in 1917. He defined it as "that most usually heard in everyday speech in the families of Southern English persons whose menfolk have been educated at the great public boarding-schools". And at the same time, I should mention about a survey that was conducted by Paul Coggle in 1993 in which he asked a group of British students to write the adjectives that came to their minds when they were listening to somebody speaking conservative RP. Their responses were as follows: formal, pompous, cold, over-precise and stiff. That means people in England have a negative attitude towards RP. If we look at the English used by the newsreaders and announcers on BBC, we find a lot of variations. It means even on BBC they are not using RP consistently. So there is nothing surprising that it is not used in India. So what should we do? A lot of scholars have been talking about International English. It is not British English and it is not American English. We are not interested in these varieties also, because how many times we are going to interact with the people of England or the U.S. Hardly are we going to do that. We are more likely to come across the people from Japan, China, Korea and the European and African countries. So, why not talk about international English which was proposed by A.C. Gimson some 50 years ago when he published an article in 1978. It has been popularized by David Crystal in his publications in the last 10 to 15 years.

I want to stress here that my discussion is mainly on this variety called International English. The other point that I want to mention is that personal experience is undoubtedly important, but they must be supported by theoretical insights. Otherwise, it will not be accepted, because if somebody conducts an experiment, writes a paper and sends it to a journal, the journal editor would definitely ask him or her for some theoretical input. Unless this requirement is met, the journal may not publish just the results of an experiment. Here I would like to tell you a joke. It is not really a joke, but a fact. A school teacher used to teach that the earth is static and the sun moves around it because that is what he saw everyday. The sun was rising in the east and setting in the west. After a long service in that school he was due for promotion. So he was asked to go for a training course. As a result, he was sent to a training college where he was taught that the sun is static and the earth moved around it. He vehemently objected to it because he believed it was the reverse. Finally the training school teacher threatened him that if he did not agree, he would not be given promotion. Then the trainee teacher's response was: "Alright, as long as I am in this training school, the sun is static and the earth is moving around. The moment I go back to my school the earth will be static and the sun will move around it". I am trying to drive home the point that it is necessary for our experiences and observations to be supported by theoretical insights. This will strengthen our arguments and that is what we will have to do.

Coming back to teaching and learning of English, mother tongue interference is definitely the most in the areas of Phonetics and Phonology. Why is it so? Because if an Indian writes something and somebody from Australia, New Zealand, England, or America writes the same, there will not be any significant difference between the grammars concerned. But if an Indian speaks and they speak, there will be a big difference. This is an area of concern, and we must concentrate on it. This is the reason for which the Oriyas speak *Englis*, Bengalis articulate *bhowels*. Telugus *audhor* books, Kannadigas listen to *ocal* music, and Hindi speakers do not distinguish between 'wine' and 'vine'; both are *wine* for them. Punjabis say /pleyər/ not /plezə(r)/ 'pleasure'. If we are going to talk about International English, we must have grounding in what is called Indian English. Some people say there is nothing called Indian English. What we have are Hinglish (Hindi English), Tinglish (Tamil English), Binglish (Bengali English), etc. It is not true. A lot of work has been done on Indian English, and it started 30 to 40 years ago. There are a quite number of publications on various aspects of Indian English today. Unless we have something called Standard Indian English, we cannot think of International English. First, let me discuss the segments of Indian English. Of course, both the vowels and consonants of British English are notorious for Indians to learn. It is because most of the well-known Indian languages have as many as eight vowels, a few or no diphthongs, no fricatives except one or two sibilants and [h]. These are the real problems which the English teachers also do not realise.

Yesterday I broached this problem, which is very common in Indian English. Once I asked one of my students from the neighbouring state West Bengal where he came from. He said "I come from *Waste* Bengal". We cannot do anything because there is no difference between "west" and "waste" in Bengali pronunciation. An Oriya speaker goes to a hairdresser and tells him: "Save me". That is how things are. Of course, when we talk about conversation in English, the distinctions between 'west' and 'waste' and 'save' and 'shave' are necessary. When a participant of this seminar was mentioning some English jokes, I felt like telling you that those jokes were in English; not in Indian English. The jokes in Indian English are different. For example, you should not wish a speaker of the Bengali language in English. If you say, "Happy new year!", that Bengali speaker should typically respond: "Shame to you". It is because the difference between /s/ and /ʃ/ is not phonemic or significant in Bengali. The second example is: don't seek the blessings of somebody from Assam. If you say 'Namaskar', he or she is likely to say "hata:yubhava" literally meaning 'Lose your life span' because Assamese speakers normally change [s] to [h]. I have heard many English Professors from Assam saying English "literasure". The third example is that most of us watch Jee TV, not Zee TV. We will have to somehow identify all those language specific interferences and do away with them in order to build a platform for Indian English. Let us take another example from English. If we count the words in English which have the sound [ʒ], we will find not more than 20 or 30 words contain this sound. But English has retained this exceptional sound for centuries. Why? This is an important question. Since English makes a distinction between /p/ and /b/, /f/ and /v/, /t/ and /d/, /θ/ and /ð/, /s/ and /z/, /k/ and /g/, etc., it also needs to make a distinction between /s/ and /ʒ/, because it is a part of the system of the English language. Even though there are only a handful of words which contain the sound [ʒ], English has retained it for so long. It is common place that if we know some 2000 English words, we should be in a position to communicate effectively with others. Now the question is: why not we make our students practise as to how to pronounce these 2000 words? The problem is that students are not machines, they are learners; and learning is not just memorization or simple storage. Whatever we learn has to be digested. Students must be in a position to formulate the rules on their own and use them while speaking English. I should try to impress upon you that Second Language Acquisition is to a great extent like First Language Acquisition. If you have observed children acquiring English as the first language, it is common for them to say "I *ated* rice", not "ate". In the next phase they say "I *eated* rice" and the third phase it becomes "I ate rice". Parents hardly correct a child when he or she acquires the mother tongue. No English speaking adult corrects his/her child when the latter says "I eated/ated rice." The child himself or herself comes across additional data with reference to how others speak the language and acquires the correct form or structure. This is what happens and a similar thing is probably necessary for us to do when we were teaching a second language like English. We all know that there are four major language skills and they are arranged in this order: listening, speaking, reading and writing. But when it comes to teaching English, we start teaching the alphabet in the very first class. That means when the child does not know anything about English, we start teaching him or her with the alphabet of English, and it is not a good way of teaching. What we are doing is that we are teaching English as it is done in England or in the United States of America because their children's mother tongue is English. When they go to school, they possess a lots of knowledge of the language. They are almost normal speakers in the English language. In India, when we teach an Indian language, we teach primarily the alphabet and the academic vocabulary and some difficult structures. Because when children come to school at the age of five they have already acquired a lot of their mother tongues. So we are not going to teach them their languages, but the script, the academic vocabulary and certain difficult structures. Of course, if a child comes from a socially disadvantaged or a dialect speakers' background, a bit of correction in his/her pronunciation is necessary. I must state here that I come from a rural background, I went to an Oriya medium school, and I speak better Oriya than many Oriyas from the urban areas and towns of Orissa.

What we are discussing here is that when we teach pronunciation we must equip the learners with enough 'input' that can be used or converted into 'intake'. It is necessary to make a distinction between 'input' and 'intake'. What the teacher teaches the student is 'input'. Unless it is converted into 'intake' teaching/learning has not taken place. Teaching has not taken place because teaching must be converted into learning. If that does not happen, then, I think, the purpose is defeated.

Now I am a little tempted to talk about the relationship between English spelling and pronunciation. I will give you two examples. The English letter 'c' is pronounced in two ways: one is [k] and the other one is [tʃ]. It is highly rule-governed. The [s] pronunciation takes place whenever 'c' is followed by 'i' 'e' as 'y', e.g. city, centre, cyber. In all the other environments 'c' is pronounced [k] e.g. cut, cot, cat, cry, clown, etc. We won't get a single example where this rule does not work. But often we do not understand such rules and say that English spelling is bizarre. A similar rule can be formulated for the letter 'g' which is realized as [g] and [dʒ] in different environments, though it is not as simple as the rule for 'c'. Take another example. The sequence 'th' is pronounced [θ] in some cases and [ð] in some other cases. We can formulate rules which work in most cases. If we consider the pronunciation [ð], it happens mostly in the function words. We can take pronouns like they, them, their, this, that and some basic adverbs like then, thus, and the definite article 'the' as evidence. We will hardly find this pronunciation in the content words, e.g. think, thought, thin, thing, etc. If we can involve the students by giving them a lot of data and encourage them to find out the rule where [θ] pronunciation takes place and where [ð] pronunciation takes place it will be of great advantage. Once they discover the rules they will be delighted and feel proud that they have been able to discover the rules. It is needless to say that this kind of feeling will encourage the children to learn more and discover more.

Another problem that I would like to bring to your notice is that there is a word 'bath' that ends in /θ/. The moment we add 'e' to it, it becomes 'bathe' that ends in /ð/. It implies that in a distant past there was no distinction between /θ/ and /ð/ in English. If we look at Old English, there was only /θ/ and [ð] was its allophone that occurred inter-vocalically or between two vowels. The same thing happened to /f/ also. Take for example, 'thief' that has /f/. In the plural form, /f/ becomes [v] because it occurs inter-vocalically, i.e. 'thieves'. What I am trying to emphasize is that the rule in English those days was that whenever a voiceless fricative occurred in between two vowels, it was pronounced as a voiced one. Later /θ/ and /ð/ became separate phonemes due to various reasons including internal phonological changes as well as borrowings from French. As a result, in Modern English we have words like 'fan' and 'van' where /f/ and /v/ contrast with each other. Even today in German, 'von' is written with 'v' but it is pronounced /f/. The sequence 'ch' has three articulations in English: /tʃ/, /ʃ/ and /k/. If we look at the language carefully, words such as cherry, cheese, church, cheap, etc. are original English words. That means in the original English words 'ch' was pronounced [tʃ] whereas in the French borrowings, especially after the Middle English period, it has become /ʃ/ e.g. champagne, chef, sachet. The third one is [k] pronunciation of the sequence 'ch'. We find that this occurs primarily in the initial position of a word, and most of these words are borrowed either from Latin or Greek. For example, chaos, character, chemistry, chord, etc. If we consider the English language from these points of view, we will find its spelling rule-governed to a great extent. Take another example, in English, the 'ie' and 'ei' sequences are problematic and students often confuse whether it is *receive* or *recieve*. That is what I see in my students' writing. I am sure you have experienced the same as teachers of English. My students who are not sure of this spelling rule put a dot above 'e' and write 'i' like 'e' so that I will give them the benefit of doubt. If they understand that after 'c' it has to be always 'e' for the [s] pronunciation, then they would definitely use the 'ei' sequence after it. In all other cases, it has to be 'ie', e.g. believe, relieve, achieve, etc. If we analyse the English spellings like this, we can discover a lot of rules.

I just want to touch upon the problem of stress in English now. We may tell our students that if it is a disyllabic noun, the first syllable is stressed, e.g. 'present. But if it is a disyllabic verb, then the second syllable is stressed, e.g. pre'sent. I should tell you an incident here that took place in Orissa almost a century ago. Nilakantha Das was a scholar, a poet, a statesman, a social reformer, and a freedom fighter. I consider him the greatest intellectual of the 20th century Orissa. He was the Principal of Satyavadi Vana Vidyalaya, a school that was established for the spread of ethics, morality, spirit of freedom, etc. One day when Das was going around the school, the English teacher was teaching the English adverbs to the students. He defined the adverb as follows: whenever you find 'ly' at the end of a word it is an adverb. But an intelligent student immediately asked him: "What about Italy? Is it an adverb?" Obviously, the teacher had no satisfactory answer, and he had to loose his job because of that. Das dismissed the teacher. It is very easy to say that if a disyllabic word is a noun, the first syllable is stressed and if it is a verb, the second syllable is stressed. Let us take 'collapse'. Whether it is used as a noun or a verb, the second syllable is always stressed. The question is: Why is it so? When we are going to teach stress, we must train students in such a way that they themselves should be in a position to formulate the related rules and find out where the stress is going to occur or should occur. I do not say that they would always determine the stress placement correctly, but I have little doubt that they would succeed in most of the cases. Now let us discuss it with appropriate examples. Take two verbs like 'exist' and 'exit'. In 'exist', the second syllable is stressed. It is because the second syllable is heavy as 'st' is a consonant cluster. Since it is heavy, it must bear the stress. On the other hand, in 'exit', the second syllable is light. Hence, the stress falls on the first syllable. The same is the case with 'collapse'. Here again there is a cluster in the end of the word, and that is why the second syllable is stressed even if it is used as a noun. We cannot pronounce 'collapse it has to be coll'apse. We can explain all these and convince the students that everything is rule-governed in a language; even in English. Of course, we will have to go a little further and discuss what is meant by heavy syllable and what is meant by light syllable, etc. It is not obligatory to talk about onset, rhyme, coda, nucleus, etc. They may be discussed, if and when required, but certainly not the details of all these and syllable division. Our effort should be to give problems to students in such a form that they themselves can come up with the rules. If we can tell them that whenever there is a heavy syllable, it is a preferred site for the placement of stress. Once children start playing with the language data, they may come up with their own rules of stress. If this is achieved, teaching will be considered highly successful. I have experimented this 'bottom-up' approach in my courses and found it to be quite useful.

Now coming back to spoken English, we find that it mostly deals with Phonetics and Phonology, and almost no grammar. This is, undoubtedly, not a good way of doing things. I will give you two examples. Take the use of "which" and "that" because many times we consider them synonymous. In fact, if we look at the usage, usually 'which' is found in the formal discourse or register whereas 'that' is found in the informal or less formal register. Let me give some examples which are used more in the academic prose. In the academic prose and news, 'which' is used very frequently whereas 'that' is found usually in conversation, plays and fiction. What I am trying to tell you is that if you are speaking to somebody informally, 'that' is preferred to 'which' as a relative pronoun. Again, I find Indians using 'got' and 'gotten' both, 'gotten' is American though I see a lot of people in India use it. Suppose you say: "Have you gotten an exam today"?, here 'gotten' is used in the sense "Do you have an exam today?". On the other hand, if somebody says "I have gotten my salary" it conveys a perfective meaning of the verb. But many times we confuse ourselves. I have heard Indian English speakers using 'got' in the place of 'gotten' and vice-versa. Again, it is not uncommon to hear an educated Indian saying "I myself has seen you coming to this place". Most probably, it is an over-generalization of 'he himself' and 'she herself'. Because of the 'self' part, we consider 'myself' like 'himself' or 'herself', in the traditional grammar terminology. It prompts us to use the verb accordingly.

When we are discussing theory and practice of English pronunciation, as a teacher we must know a little bit of theory, otherwise it will be very difficult for us to answer the questions students are going to ask. There are some students who are really intelligent and they ask questions that are very hard to answer. If we do not have a theoretical base, it will be very difficult to answer the questions satisfactorily. I will give you one example: one day a student asked me: "Is it 'walking distance' or 'walkable distance'"? He said that he used 'walkable distance'; but another person told him 'walking distance' was correct. Instead of giving a straight answer, I gave him some examples. As mentioned earlier, I believe in and practise the bottom-up approach in teaching. If we follow the top-down approach, i.e. give the definition first and then give examples, I doubt if the students are going to learn that very part well. I always give them a lot of data and allow them to discover the rules so that they derive pleasure of discovering something new. So I asked the student: Is it 'walking stick' or 'walkable stick'? He answered 'walking stick'. Then I said: "Is it 'sinking ship' or 'sinkable ship'"? He said: "Sinking ship". Notice here that whenever we have such structures that have 'running', 'walking', 'sinking', etc. the noun plays the subject role, i.e. the ship which sinks, the stick which walks (with the person). But it is the reverse in the case of 'walkable'. The noun 'distance' is the object in 'walkable distance'. I was delighted to that student's eyes glowing and he wore a smile of satisfaction on his face.

Thank you very much for this opportunity and a very patient hearing.

References

Coggle, Pul. 1993. *Do You Speak Estuary English?* London: Bloomsbury Publishing Ltd.

Crystal, David. 2003. *English as a Global Language*. Cambridge: Cambridge University Press (First published in 1997).

Gimson, A.C. 1978. "Towards an international pronunciation of English". In: *In Honour of A.S. Hornby*, Ed. Peter Strevens. Oxford: Oxford University Press.

Jones, Daniel. 2003. *Cambridge English Pronunciation Dictionary*. Cambridge: Cambridge University Press (first published in 1917).

Contributors

Sudhakar Marathe, Former Dean and Professor, Department of English, School of Humanities, University of Hyderabad, Hyderabad-500 046.

D. Murali Manohar, Associate Professor in English, Department of English, University of Hyderabad, Hyderabad-500 046. E-mail: dmbm_vs@yahoo.co.in

V. Prasad, P.G.T. English, Jawahar Navodaya Vidyalaya, Kalapet, Puducherry-605 014.

Durga Prasad Dash, Asst. Professor in English, GMR Institute of Technology, At/Po-Rajam, Dist-Srikakulam (AP).

Sharda Acharya, Lecturer in English, Silicon Institute of Technology, Bhubaneswar-751 024.

Trishna Kar, Lecturer in English, Gandhi Institute for Technology, Gramadiha, Bubaneswar-752 054.

Sreedevi G. Mahapatra, P.G.T. English, Jawahar Navodaya Vidyalaya, Kommadi, Visakhapatnam, Andhra Pradesh-530 048.

Susanto, Ph.D. Participant in Linguistics and Phonetics, English and Foreign Languages (EFL) University, Hyderabad-Andhra Pradesh. E-mail: susantonanda@gmail.com

A. Mallikarjunappa, Dept. of English, Veerashaiva College, Bellary-583 104, Karnataka. E-mail: mallik_59@yahoo.co.in

Aswini Kumar Mishra, Asst. Professor, S.V. Institute of Engineering & Technology, Ethabar Pally, Moinabad, Hyderabad.

Arabati Pradeep Kumar, Asst. Professor in English, H. No. 8-5-281, Laxminagar, Karimnagar-505 001, Andhra

Pradesh. E-mail: pranavkoundinya@gmail.com, pradeep_a_kumar@yahoo.com

Mousumi Dash, Lecturer in English, ITER, S'O'A University, Bhubaneswar.

Monalisa Mishra, Lecturer in English, ITER, S'O'A University, Bhubaneswar.

R.V. Jayanth Kasyap, Asst. Professor in English, Yogi Vemana University, Kadapa, Andhra Pradesh.

E. Vijaya Raghava, M.Phil. Scholar, Dept. of English University of Hyderabad, Hyderabad; Director, Victory English Institution, Mehdipatnam, Hyderabad.

P. Hari Padma Rani, Associate Professor in English, Head, Department of English, Sri Padmavati Mahila Viswa Vidyalaya, Tirupati.

Srinivasa Kumar Kolusu, Ph.D. Participant, Dept. of Dravidian & Computational Linguistics, Dept. of materials Production, Dravidian University, Kuppam. E-mail: kumarksrini@gmail.com

Anand Mahanand, Asst. Professor, Dept. of Materials Production, English and Foreign Languages University, Hyderabad.

Suchismita Barik, M.Phil English Scholar, School of English Language Education, EFL University, Hyderabad.

R. Dyvadatham, Dept. of English & Communications, ITER, S'O'A University, Dravidian University, Kuppam-517 425. E-mail: pra30sad@yahoo.com

B. Bhujanga Reddy, Asst. Professor, Department of Telugu, University of Hyderabad, Hyderabad-500 046. E-mail: bbreddy65@gmail.com

Sridhar Maisa, Ph.D. Scholar, Department of English, University of Hyderabad, Hyderabad.

Panchanan Mohanty, Professor, Centre for Applied Linguistics and Translation Studies, University of Hyderabad, Hyderabad-500 046. E-mail: panchanan_mohanty@ yahoo.com